a sneaking
suspicion

by John Dickson

For Rob and Jaime—
my brothers and friends.

A Sneaking Suspicion
Fourth edition
© Matthias Media 2004

First edition 1992
Second edition 1994
Third edition 1999

Matthias Media
(St Matthias Press Ltd ACN 067 558 365)
PO Box 225
Kingsford NSW 2032
Australia
Telephone: (02) 9663 1478; international: +61-2-9663-1478
Facsimile: (02) 9663 3265; international: +61-2-9663-3265
Email: info@matthiasmedia.com.au
Internet: www.matthiasmedia.com.au

Matthias Media (USA)
Telephone: 724 964 8152; international: +1-724-964-8152
Facsimile: 724 964 8166; international: +1-724-964-8166
Email: sales@matthiasmedia.com
Internet: www.matthiasmedia.com

Scripture quotations are taken from the CONTEMPORARY ENGLISH VERSION (CEV). Copyright © American Bible Society 1991. Used by permission.

The poem 'Death Lib' from *Up To Date* by Steve Turner is quoted on p. 88. Copyright Hodder & Stoughton Ltd. Used by permission.

ISBN 978 1 876326 90 6

Illustrations © Chris Morgan www.cxmedia.com.
Design and typesetting by Matthias Media.

Other publications by John Dickson:
A Hell of a Life
Hanging in There
If I were God, I'd end all the pain
If I were God, I'd make myself clearer
Simply Christianity: A modern guide to the ancient faith

John can be contacted in cyberspace care of: jdickson@matthiasmedia.com.au

Contents

Part 3: The guts of it all

Introduction

You might agree that Australians on the whole have never been a particularly religious bunch. When church attendance was made compulsory in the 1790s, the early settlers responded by burning Australia's first and only church building to the ground.

Some people have referred to this church burning incident as symbolic of how Aussies have felt about religion right up to today. Part of me agrees with this. You've only got to read the mags, watch the TV and listen to the radio to learn that one of the most consistent pictures of a 'religious' person is a narrow-minded nerd who wears sandals over his socks, eats all his veggies, and goes to bed by nine o'clock every night. This modern parody of Christianity is not as violent as torching a church but it is every bit as effective at keeping the average 'normal' Australian at arms length from religion.

And yet despite the apparent cynicism towards religion, there have always been real signs that Australians are not the 'church-burning pagans' they might at first appear to be. I'm always getting into conversations about spiritual things with people I meet at parties—and it's hardly ever me who brings it up. It usually starts with someone asking, "What do you do with your time?" I usually explain that I spend close to half of my year writing books about big things like 'faith', 'God', 'life' and 'death'. No sooner have I said this than the person tells me the story of their spiritual life. They tell me about the good experiences and the bad ones. They explain what they don't like about formal religion but do like about the 'bloke upstairs'. Suddenly, someone who doesn't normally talk much

7

about spiritual stuff has told me his or her theory on life, the universe and everything. Nine times out of ten people admit to having a sneaking suspicion there's something 'out there'; they just aren't too sure what it is exactly. Perhaps you're the same. Perhaps you too have a 'hunch' that there is a spiritual side to life—a quiet feeling that what we see and hear in the media is not the whole picture.

The big question is: can we ever see the whole picture?

Is it possible to find a path through all the ideas, trends and religions in modern life? Can we hope to ever have more than a hunch about God? In a way, this book attempts to paint the picture from one angle: the Christian angle.

In a multicultural society, Christianity is only one of many ways of looking at life, but each of the following chapters hopes to show that the more you compare the message of Christ with other ideas, the more convincing it becomes. A book like this is not going to change the world, but it may just help to confirm some of your own suspicions about life, love, sex, death and God. That's my hope, anyway.

John Dickson
August 2004

PS. Special thanks to Tim Baldwin for helping with the updates for this new edition.

PART 1

some sneaking
suspicions

1

The sex factor

IS SEX MORE LIKE A PORSCHE THAN A DATSUN?

It might seem strange to start this book by talking about sex, but it seemed to me that wherever I put this chapter, you'd probably have read it first anyway (I know I would). So to save you the trouble, I've put it first.

Before Madonna was the respectable mother-figure of the music scene, she put out a movie that was probably designed to shock. One scene of *In Bed With Madonna* was especially interesting.

During one of her onstage performances, a huge bed appears on stage. Madonna slips into sexual overdrive and begins rolling around the bed in a display of not-so-subtle sensuality. Her dancers also get excited, rubbing their bodies against hers and stroking the hot spots, so to speak. All this, to the words, "Like a virgin, touched for the very first time".

As you can well imagine, everyone is having a great time—Madonna, the dancers, the concert audience and those watching the film. Everyone except the Canadian police. In the film, we watch the men-in-uniform rock up to the 20,000 seat concert hall with a demand: cut that naughty scene or be 'shut down'. Madonna's promoters are genuinely worried and scurry up to her dressing room and tell her the bad news. She thinks for a moment and decides to ignore the police demands for 'decency' and go on with the show as planned. In this case, the 'express yourself' mentality wins the day.

This scene in the film illustrates two directly opposite attitudes toward sex.

1. Sex is naughty. Ban it.

2. Sex is wonderful. Flaunt it.

I'm assuming you're an average human being like me, so we don't really need to spend any time discussing the flaws in the first view. It's negative, boring and denies the obvious fact that humans are sexual creatures.

But to be honest, I'm concerned that the 'flaunt it' approach is dangerous, cheap and is ultimately a rip-off (so to speak). Let me explain.

Sexperts

The 'experts' on sex, or 'sexperts' for short, are everywhere in our society, all of them offering advice on this important topic. You'll find them on TV, on radio and, if the number of pages is anything to go by, teen mags would have to be the most expert of the lot. And what's the message of the mags? Although the photos change from article to article the main point never changes—if you want to do it, just do it, but do it safe!

Then there's Sydney's Gay and Lesbian Mardi Gras. Surely if anyone knows how to bring sex to the masses it's these guys and gals. It's the largest annual 'cultural' event in Australia, and it's all about sex. There's groovy music, bright costumes, risqué choreography, and a message that booms out loud and clear to the whole country—sex is about the freedom to do and be whatever you want!

And of course the movies can bring us the closest thing to the real thing in full technicolour and surround sound. In fact, with the help of gorgeous actors, stirring background music and the big screen, what they deliver is even better than the real thing. And what is the message of the movie sexperts? The best sex happens when you're beautiful and not married (at least not married to the person you want to have the best sex with)!

Take the movie *The People vs. Larry Flynt* as an example. Larry Flynt was the editor of *Hustler*, one of the world's top selling men's magazines. He is also rated as one of the great sexual 'heroes' of the 20th century. In the movie Larry is this heroic businessman who has to fight against the intolerance and self-righteousness of some sections of American society. Larry has a life full of excitement, pleasure and most of all, freedom. That's until some closed-minded bigot shoots him. Our hero now has to spend the rest of his life in a wheelchair, paralyzed. Larry is more than a hero. He's a martyr—someone who sacrifices so much in his fight for sexual freedom. That's how the movie goes, anyway.

But if you scratch beneath the surface of all the hype you

find some pretty interesting facts. Turns out the real Flynt was by many reports just a greedy businessman with an insatiable sexual appetite; an appetite that has led to all sorts of allegations against him concerning sleazy, oppressive and demeaning sexual activity. His own daughter was protesting outside the opening night begging people not to believe the lie presented in the film.

Finding this out made me realize that the Larry Flynt story is a good example of what's true of nearly all our modern sexperts. On the surface they seem to be the great promoters and freedom-fighters for sex, but when you scratch beneath the beautifully glossy surface, it's just the opposite. The promoters turn out to be demoters; their fight doesn't bring freedom, it sets a trap, which many of us fall into.

The teen mags aren't really interested in giving advice that will lead to the best sex life. They tell us what they think we want to hear, so that we'll keep buying the magazine, so that advertisers will keep buying advertising space, so that they'll keep making money (remember, many of these magazines have more advertising managers than writers on their staff). If they thought you wanted to hear, "Be celibate!", that's exactly what they'd be saying. Although they go on and on about sex, they don't appear to value sex at all, except as a way of selling magazines.

Kevin Williamson, a major TV and movie producer (*Dawson's Creek, Scream, Cursed*), claims: "We present sexual issues without any judgements, we don't preach, we just show teens talking about what's important to them". In reality though, most TV shows (including his) do preach; they just do it in a slick and subtle way. Beneath the expensive exterior, people like Williamson are just peddling the same cheap message: If it feels good, do it! Just do it safe!

The same is true of the movies and the Mardi Gras. On the surface they look like they're fighting for sexual freedom, but beneath the gloss and volume it turns out that they're really promoting sexual selfishness, triviality and unfaithfulness.

Here's some examples of what I mean.

One of those attractive blonde 'singers' (whose name we easily forget) had a hit single some time back in which the key lyric said: "Do to me what your eyes say you want to do. Do it, read my lips."

I've often wondered what would happen if this young woman went to a few high schools I know and said to the blokes, "Boys, do to me what your eyes say you want to do". Most girls wouldn't dream of letting blokes do even half of what our hormone-blurred eyes say we want to do—sorry blokes!

Or then there's the effort by Justin Timberlake, 'Take me Now'. In it he sings, "I'm hungry for your loving; You got me working, honey; I'm hot just like an oven; So take me now". Here 'loving' is reduced to being 'taken'. I reckon if I said this to my wife, after laughing at me she'd probably hit me. So she should.

And as for the song by Nickelback I have in front me … well maybe we shouldn't lower the tone any further.

Anyway, I expect these 'singers' don't really mean everything they sing, but it makes me wonder why they'd bother with such obviously cheap words. I guess you can justify anything if it sells a few CDs.

The Family Planning Association of NSW once sponsored a diary called the *Fact and Fantasy File*, which they said was designed to make you "better informed about your own body, sex and relationships". The diary, and an associated sex-info telephone hotline, was banned by the government. But not before a couple of thousand copies of the book got out to school students, nurses and me.

I think I read it with a fairly open mind, but I must say I was under-impressed. It wasn't the explicit details that concerned me (I am a married man). It was the cheap picture of sex that the authors painted. For a group that wanted to promote sex, they did a very poor job. For example, how's this for a poem about sexual intimacy?

Love is great
Love is golden
Love is made
In the back of a Holden

And the handy sex tip for March 13th is sure to please your partner:

If you find sex boring, thinking about other things that make you sexually excited during intercourse can heighten the experience.

Imagine your reaction when, during an intimate moment, you discover that your partner is fantasizing about someone other than you. I don't know about you, but I'd feel pretty humiliated and jealous, and any sense of intimacy would be lost in an instant. This sort of fantasizing may 'heighten the experience' of pleasure but not of the whole sexual encounter nor, more importantly, the relationship of trust between two people.

One episode of the TV series *Sex* gave similar advice. It encouraged us to fantasize as much as we like during sex but just keep it to ourselves so as not to hurt our partner's feelings. Sounds fine if you're only in it for the physical encounter. However, most of us agree that sex is meant to be the expression of a relationship. Relationships are built on loyalty and honesty, not mental unfaithfulness and deceit.

Unfortunately though, some of us are influenced by these

views. In a *Girlfriend* magazine article entitled, 'Let's Talk About Sex', a survey was conducted asking teenage girls about their sexual views. One worrying point in particular was made. It read that in deciding when to have sex, 66% of the girls surveyed said "they came to a mutual decision ... they both felt it was the right thing to do". The magazine then concluded by saying this was "a very sensible decision". The problem with 'feeling' it's the right thing to do is that many blokes feel it's right any time! The warm fuzzies of new love, combined with the strong drive of the sexual urge, are not reliable indicators for such important decision making.

These are just a few of the many, many examples in modern society where sex is discussed without mention of relationships. It's as if physical pleasure is all that there is to sex. As soon as we accept the advice of these 'sexperts' we're heading for a hollow, confusing and even harmful view of sex—one that threatens to ruin our relationships. We'll end up wondering why on earth we can't hold down a romantic friendship, and why commitment, trust and honesty are so foreign to our relationships. It's an undersell—a rip-off.

Porsche or Datsun

In all the wide discussion, debate and argument about condom machines in schools, AIDS, abortion and homosexuality, I've been amazed at how little is being said about the intimate side of sex.

In the *Girlfriend* article just mentioned they also reported that, after having sex, most girls in their survey "felt really close to their boyfriends". This is not surprising.

Any psychologist, sex therapist or average person on the street will tell you that a sexual encounter is often a 'whole person' encounter. By this I mean that there is an emotional and psychological impact which accompanies sexual intercourse. It's not just a physical act, like going to the toilet. It touches deep emotions. It is this 'deeper' dimension to sex that many of us are being conned out of.

My first car was an orange Datsun 1200. It got me from A to B, but it really was a rust bucket. It only cost me a thousand bucks, so I didn't treat it too well and had no problem lending it out to any of my friends. I figured that if they crashed it, it was no big deal. Suppose though, I owned a Porsche 968. I can assure you, I'd care for it with my life and certainly wouldn't lend it out. In my mind, such a valuable machine deserves the utmost care. But what's this got to do with sex and relationships?

The media 'sexperts' can fool us into believing a Datsun view of sex. Lend it out. It's not that special. But in God's eyes, sex is more like a Porsche. It is valuable. It demands care. It is something precious to us (and to him), not merely the machinery by which we get about and enjoy ourselves.

If humans were just glorified apes who wear Nikes, then it probably makes sense to live entirely by our 'natural' instincts. However, if there is something different about us humans, if relationships are a vital key to our fulfilment, if there is a God who has carefully designed a plan for our sexual lives, then it makes sense to preserve our expression of sexual intimacy until we find a partner with whom lifelong commitment, loyalty and trust have meaning.

Far from being against sex, God is very much for it. It's not as if Adam and Eve discovered sex one day and thought, "Oops, let's not tell God. He's bound to get annoyed." Remember, the Creator is creative. He could have invented a method of having kids that involved spitting on each other's big toe, if he had wanted to. But instead, he invented sex—fantastic, enjoyable, intimate and exciting. And because sex is so valuable, God has given some very smart guidelines and rules for its enjoyment and to keep us from getting hurt and from hurting others. The so called 'sexperts' usually say these guidelines are restrictive and boring, but that might just be because they have been tricked into thinking that the 'Porsche' is a 'Datsun'.

Actually, God's insistence that we enjoy sex in the context of a lifelong relationship of loyalty and trust is the most liberating and meaningful sexpert advice around. When you're in bed with someone who has promised to devote their life to you for keeps, the experience is so much better. For a start there is a deep, mutual trust—something that is essential for great sex, and near impossible to find in a casual sexual relationship. More than that, because you're with your life-time partner, you have all the time in the world to get better and better at enjoying each other physically. The desire to get what you want while you can (a very selfish and unsatisfying approach to sex) gives way to a desire to give all you can for as long as you can (a very satisfying approach to sex). The pressure to 'perform' (something that often hinders 'performance') gives way to mutual acceptance and enjoyment of each other (something that often heightens 'performance'). The list of the benefits of God's rules about sex could go on and on.

The point of no return

Unlike today, in first-century Palestine (when Jesus was alive), sexual immorality was a very big deal. A true story is recorded in the Bible about a woman who was known to have "lived a sinful life in that town". There are no prizes for guessing what people meant by that phrase. One day Jesus happened to be in town having a meal at the home of a prominent religious leader named Simon and this woman turned up. Now, it was bad enough for a normal person to turn up without an invitation, so imagine what it was like for a woman with her reputation. To make things worse, she came into the room, fell down at Jesus' feet and burst into tears. Imagine the scene now. Here was this woman in all her fear and shame in a room full of self-righteous religious people. As you'd expect, Simon was furious, not only with the woman but also with Jesus. He thought to himself, if Jesus really was a man sent from God he'd be able to tell what kind of woman she was and would tell her to back off. But the point is this: Jesus did know what kind of woman she was and still welcomed her. In fact, Jesus even defended her in front of all these important guests. To top it all off, he then turned to her and spoke what must have been the kindest words she had heard for a long time: "Your sins are forgiven". I'm sure she could hardly believe her ears. She had been used to guilt and rejection, but here was someone offering her acceptance and forgiveness. These words marked a new beginning in her life.

I suppose some of you are aware of the big rip-off that robs sex of intimacy and leaves us with a cheap substitute. Some of you have experienced it first hand. When I read this story and others like it (the Bible is full of them), I am strongly reminded that in Jesus' mind there is no such thing as a 'point of no return'. No matter what we've done or become, the great news is that there can be restoration, forgiveness and a new beginning.

For suspicious minds

1. What attitudes about sex do you think you've absorbed from movies and the media? Do you think these are accurate?
2. Would you describe your attitude to sex as a 'Porsche' or a 'Datsun'?
3. Does God's attitude to sex make sense to you?

4. Try reading the story about Jesus and the sexually immoral woman. You'll find it in Luke, chapter 7, starting at verse 36. If you were this 'sinful' woman, what impact on your life would this meeting with Jesus have?

2

The beauty myth

HAVE I GOT 'THE LOOK' OR HAS IT GOT ME?

A few years ago, I was touring in Adelaide with the band I used to sing for. After one of our shows, I was walking through the almost empty concert hall when I passed a girl in a wheelchair.

"Excuse me, can we talk please?" she said in very slurred speech.

"Sure we can", I replied and grabbed a chair to sit down.

For the next half an hour or so, she explained her story. She had been in a serious car accident with some friends and had been severely injured. For the first 11 weeks, she was in a coma and it was not clear what her situation would be. When she eventually came out of the coma, the doctors realized that she had lost her ability to walk, talk and write. She remained in hospital for many more months and recovery was slow. The night I met her, she was still unable to walk but her speech was improving steadily. Her name was Tiffany. She was 18.

As she told me this story, I was really quite disturbed and moved. I asked if we could keep in touch, and so she reached into her handbag, pulled out a couple of photos of herself and began scribbling her name and address on the back of one of them. I took the photos, looked at them and could hardly believe my eyes. They were shots taken just before the accident. They were modelling shots. She was beautiful.

As I said goodbye, I couldn't help thinking of all that she had lost—her modelling ambitions, friends and her fair share of guys, as you might imagine. Strangely, though, she doesn't quite see her situation like that. For all her loss, she also feels she has 'gained'. Her letters to me since that time contain some of the most uplifting and positive things you could hope to read. This tragic experience has taught her things which I think many of us need to learn if we are to know anything about true happiness. She has discovered that the most valuable things in life are 'inside qualities', not 'outside images'.

I'll come back to Tiffany later in the chapter. I wanted to tell you her story because meeting her has caused me to do a lot of thinking about what has recently been described as 'the beauty myth'.

As I'm writing this, about 10 copies of various teenage and

fashion magazines lie at my feet—not mine, of course, it's just research for the book! Browsing at the front covers, one topic steals the limelight—*image*.

Here are some front cover headlines:

Keep it off! How not to be fat at thirty

20 essentials for dressing like a model

Haircuts that could change your life

Fashion with passion

Fashion conscious teenagers are not the only ones who are into image. In the *Sydney Morning Herald*, I found an advertisement for a business seminar on how to dress. Here's part of the ad:

Successful people know that you must look good to succeed ... You always make some kind of statement with the way you dress, powerful or inept ... People think that the way they dress doesn't really matter. But it really does. The most public thing about you is the way you look. Dress right—get what you want ... Come and find out how you can get whatever you want through your image ... Dressing To Win in only one afternoon you can change your life ... It's only $95.

You don't have to be a social psychologist to work out that, in Australia, the quest for 'the look' is an obsession.

Of course, there is nothing at all wrong with wanting to look good. All of us appreciate beauty. I love the fact that my wife looks so good people wonder how on earth she ended up with me. However, in my opinion something very dangerous is happening right across Australian (male and female) society.

Role models

It's a real concern that for many people *looking* good is the same as *being* good. It's possible to have such an unhealthy emphasis on our outside appearance that the 'inside' wastes away.

On almost every page of the popular teenage magazines, there is some hot-looking girl or some gorgeous-looking guy advertising or modelling something. There's nothing wrong with this—the magazine wouldn't sell if it had you and me in it. The problem is that we are left with a strong impression of 'the essential look' and we attempt to imitate it. Unfortunately, for most of us, 'the look' is often so far out of reach that we live in constant frustration, never quite making it. In Naomi Wolf's book, *The Beauty Myth*, she says that in recent times "the weight of models plummeted to 23 percent below that of ordinary women". That means that if, for example, the average woman weighed a healthy 65 kilograms, the average model would be an unhealthy 14.95 kilograms less.

Try an exercise next time you're in a bus or some other public place. Look through your favourite magazine, choose 10 pictures at random and see how many of them you would consider to have 'the look'. Then glance up and down the bus, count 10 people at random and see how they compare. This may sound like a silly thing to do, but it does show that the fashion world has very little in common with reality. And what's worse, these fashion models become role models.

What happens when a 16-year-old girl pores over her magazines, watches the beauties on MTV, fantasizes about her own *Extreme Makeover*, and then peers in the mirror? What happens when she wants to look like her favourite model (now her role model) but simply can't? Well, for most people, it's no major drama. For others though, it becomes a driving, even desperate obsession. Moods swing up and down. Attractive friends turn into 'cows' and envy, jealousy and back-stabbing take over.

According to one survey, every day 67% of women feel

guilty about eating, 73% envy another woman's body, and 58% feel depressed about their weight. One slim teenage girl even said,

> I don't know how long I can go on living like this. Even when friends go on diets, I become very insecure, hoping that they won't lose weight or become thinner than me.

The look that kills

In some ways, mood swings and bitchiness are the less harmful side of the quest for beauty. There is a far more frightening aspect.

Recently, there has been a fair bit of media coverage about eating disorders. Anorexia and bulimia are two 'diseases' that are literally enslaving and destroying thousands of young girls' (and some guys') lives.

Anorexia can be described as an obsessive, self-induced starvation program, motivated by the fear of becoming fat. Bulimia is an abnormal craving for food followed by some form of purging, such as self-induced vomiting.

Recent studies indicate that about one in every 10 Australian women aged 14-20 have some form of eating disorder. For some it is their death. This is no joke. What begins as a pursuit of the 'body beautiful' can end up destroying the body altogether.

There are, of course, less severe consequences of these two diseases. Physical and mental fitness can be dramatically reduced, periods can be missed, and some women so mess up their internals that they are unable to bear children. This is not to mention the psychological impact. The quest for the right look can become an all-consuming paranoia that fills almost every thought and motivates almost every action.

It's important to note that blokes are not immune to the

Beauty Myth either (although I guess we should call it the 'Hunk Myth'). A recent report revealed "an extensive black market for steroids in gyms and high schools". Apparently, "the drugs are being used for cosmetic, not competitive, purposes". In the *Good Weekend* there was a cover article entitled, 'Selling by Male'. In it they commented:

> Those bodies that Australian men have been proud to ignore—
> that they filled with nicotine, alcohol and meat pies—are
> suddenly in the spotlight, and everyone ... is staring. Regardless
> of when Australian men lost their comfy cardigan image, the
> muscle movement is here, it's gathering momentum and its
> consequences are only too familiar to women.

I must admit, I don't know how many times I've driven past the famous Tontine sheets ad (with a muscle-bound bloke stretched out on the bed), and tried to distract Buff from looking (and comparing!). Shows like *Queer Eye for the Straight Guy* don't help either. Most of the blokes I know don't even look as good as the 'before' shots on that show—and yet apparently they've got to improve. Sure, quite a few of us could lose a little weight, and perhaps wash our hair more often, but the obsession with 'body sculpting', skin tone, and so on, sets a superficial and unrealistic standard of what makes a bloke a bloke.

Whether with girls or blokes, the fashion industry has set such an unhealthy standard that those who try to imitate virtually any popular model of today are bound for trouble.

Blame

Let me emphasize again that wanting to look your best is very normal and healthy. I hope that nothing I have said seems to condemn girls who try to look good. That is not my intention or opinion. A couple of my own friends have been victims of both anorexia and bulimia and I do not blame them. So, who is to blame? Is anyone?

In *The Beauty Myth*, Naomi Wolf argues that men are to blame. She believes that the unhealthy standards in the fashion industry are created by men to make the average woman feel bad about herself and never up to scratch. Wolf calls it a form of 'social control', similar to the way the stereo-typical image of the 'woman in the kitchen' kept women under control in the 1950s.

One problem with Wolf's theory is this: If men started the Beauty Myth, who started the Hunk Myth? Women? Besides, studies show that what most men consider to be the perfect body is quite a bit 'fatter' than the body envied by most women. One study asked a group of men and women to observe photos of different sized girls and to judge whether the girls were overweight, underweight or perfect. The result was very interesting. The girl judged as 'perfect' by 80% of women was judged as 'underweight' by 80% of men. The girl judged as 'perfect' by more than 60% of men was judged as 'overweight' by 85% of women.

This was illustrated to me some time ago when I saw a film in which one of the scenes involved a close up of the lead actress's legs. Instantly a murmur came across the cinema—girls whispering to one another the word … 'cellulite'. The blokes just saw a great pair of legs.

Although it is true that many of us guys need to be careful not to place unfair (and unhealthy) expectations on our female friends, it seems a little far fetched to place the blame for the Beauty Myth on men. It seems to me there are two other factors which contribute to our obsession with having the right look.

The first factor is an obvious one—the fashion and media industries.

Cleo recently published an article on dieting and eating disorders. In it were a couple of very interesting remarks:

By [modern] standards, Marilyn Monroe's perfect 50s body now looks like the 'before' picture in a weight-loss story.

Although said humorously, this comment is sadly true. Fashion models in the 50s were on average only 8% below that of the ordinary woman. As previously mentioned, now that figure is 23%. Interestingly, even Cleo had the honesty to admit that, "Fashion has something to answer for here". When I read this I thought, "But aren't you one of the fashion leaders of this country?" On the one hand, they preach that fashion can be held to blame, and yet in the same issue their pages are filled with exceedingly thin models.

One of the strategies of the fashion industry is this: If you see an item of clothing on a body you wish could be yours, you are more likely to buy the item. It's this 'I want to be like her/him' desire in us that makes the money for the industry. For this to work, the model must always be 'better' than you or me—more beautiful, more sexy and thinner. Now all this sounds obvious and quite reasonable, but if the models we try to imitate are always one or two steps ahead of us where will it lead?

If you can find a fashion magazine from the 50s or simply watch an old Hollywood film, compare the models and film stars with those of today. There are exceptions of course, but generally there has been a gradual 'thinning' of the ideal girl. If the Calvin Klein style of model is any indication, it's already leading down a very sad path.

The fashion industry may not have begun the beauty myth, but it certainly promotes it.

Having said this about the fashion industry I still think

there is another, more powerful factor contributing to our obsession with the look. That is, many of us have been tricked into thinking small. Or as a government *Commission For The Future* on Australian culture report put it:

> Robbed of a broader meaning to our lives, we appear to have entered an era of mass obsession, usually with ourselves: our appearance, our health and fitness.

Let me try and illustrate what I mean. Imagine if somehow I was able to trick you into thinking that the room you are now in is all there is to reality. Nothing else exists. What do you think would happen? After the initial shock you would undoubtedly begin to focus only on those things in the room—the painting, the clock, the carpet or whatever. Eventually, your whole life would revolve around the things in the room because you believe nothing else exists.

What if a similar thing happened in society at large? What if the media, fashion industry, education, family and friends somehow convinced us that there was nothing more to life than being popular, owning the right clothes and having the right body shape. What do you think might happen? It seems to me that what would happen is exactly what has happened. We'd lose sight of the big things in life and become obsessed with the small. Maybe our constant desire to have 'the look' is one example of thinking small.

The question is, then, is there something more?

Now there was no 33-billion-dollar-a-year diet industry in first-century Palestine. There wasn't even a 20-billion-dollar-a-year cosmetic industry. But the following wise words of Jesus show his timeless significance:

> Therefore I tell you, do not worry about your life, what you will eat;

or about your body, what you will wear. Life is more than food, and the body more than clothes ... But seek his [God's] kingdom, and these things will be given to you as well. Do not be afraid, little flock, for your father has been pleased to give you the kingdom. (Luke 12:22-23, 31-32)

According to Jesus, there is 'something more' to life than meets the eye. That 'something' he calls God's kingdom. It's not so much a place but a particular relationship between God and his human family—a relationship where God is king, and you and I are his children.

It is this 'kingdom' that brought a new dimension to life for my friend Tiffany (I mentioned her earlier) whose modelling dreams were cut short by a severe accident.

I was amazed to discover that while she was in hospital, she became convinced that there was indeed a God who cared for her and valued her life. She became a Christian. No, things did not get better overnight and she still has many difficulties. She occasionally gets depressed and from time to time she really misses her old life. What she did gain though, was valuable beyond description. She gained perspective, a larger view of life. Once she thought looking beautiful was the same as being fulfilled. She now sees how hollow that was. She now knows there are far richer things to live for. To use the analogy I just mentioned about being tricked into believing only in the room, it's like she's discovered the door into the beautiful outside world.

Here is part of a letter she wrote to me a while ago. Notice what it is that motivates and enriches her life.

I couldn't possibly be angry at God. God gave me another go at life, to make a better person of myself. I feel privileged to be chosen to tell young kids about God and let them know of the great and marvellous things he has done in my life.

"Great and marvellous things"—really? Is living for other people and for God personally fulfilling? I know she would answer with a resounding " *Yes!*" To Tiffany, beauty is enjoyable, but if it's not matched by 'inside qualities', such as peace, fulfilment and concern for others, it's a hollow and small approach to life.

Tiffany has discovered a beauty that lasts beyond the whims of fashion, and has learnt to accept herself. She has also discovered the wonder of knowing she is accepted by God, in whose eyes she and Elle McPherson are on precisely the same level. Tiffany sought and found the kingdom.

Of course, you don't have to be a prospective model, like Tiffany, to be tricked into thinking small. The Beauty/Hunk Myth is a dangerous half-truth that can fool us all in varying degrees. You don't have to end up in a wheelchair either before you see through it. God's kingdom is open to everyone. If we believe that "life is more than food and the body more than clothes" I guess the next obvious question is, will we take Jesus' advice and "seek his kingdom"?

For suspicious minds

1. Do you tend to think that looking good is the same as being good?
2. How do you feel about your own appearance?
3. Can you relate to the story of Tiffany? How do you think you would react in her situation?

Rated R

WHATEVER HAPPENED TO RIGHT AND WRONG?

Not too long ago, *Cleo* magazine had a list of 'What's In/What's Out' for the coming year. I was interested to see that 'guilt' came in at number 3 for the most 'out of fashion' things in modern Australia. They then added that guilt was a most 'unnecessary feeling'.

There seems to be a trend in our society to minimise the notion of right and wrong, good and evil, innocent and guilty. Instead, there are a lot of people selling (and sadly a lot of people buying) the idea that 'morality' is like bad fashion— wouldn't be seen dead wearing it.

So, once upon a time, society seriously believed that adultery was wrong. Now it's called 'an affair' and finds itself in the plot of top-selling movies. Divorce was once looked down upon as a destructive evil but now we're too sophisticated to be so judgemental. In fact, it's not called 'divorce' any more but 'a dissolution of marriage'—harder to say, but it sounds nicer. In years gone by, mass murderers were considered 'evil' and were locked away for life or executed. Now, they find good lawyers who find good psychiatrists to argue they are only 'mentally ill'. The school drug pusher who makes a profit by destroying lives is too often known as 'the cool' in many schools. The hero of many movies is now determined by how many girls he can lay and how many people he can beat up or blow away in 90 minutes of full-tilt entertainment.

I'm not against divorcees and I'm not arguing for capital punishment. I still listen to rock music and watch films. I am simply trying to illustrate that on the surface it seems as though people don't care much about right and wrong, and anyone who stands up for what is right is blasted as arrogant. If someone speaks against something calling it wrong, we say they're too judgemental, or worse, 'old-fashioned'.

So maybe *Cleo* was right when it declared that guilt is an outdated, unnecessary feeling. Personally, I'm not convinced.

The interesting thing about all this is that most of the people I've met in schools, unis and prisons do have a gut feeling about what is right and wrong. Most of us still have a hunch that there are real limits to how far we should go.

Despite *Cleo*, many of us do know and feel guilt from time to time. Regardless of how much the media sells the idea that we're free to do what we like any old time, the average person on the street seems to instinctively know otherwise. Some us may get sucked into acting like there's no right and wrong, but very few of us really believe it.

This 'gut feeling' about right and wrong is frequently demonstrated to me in school seminars. I once asked a bunch of Year 10 students to imagine their life story—everything they'd done, said and thought—on film, in high definition and surround sound. I asked them what rating their film would get. Some of the young blokes yelled out, "Oh, rated R!", and "Rated X!" I then said something like, "Imagine if God could see your life's film, everything you'd ever done, said and thought, and decided to hold the bad stuff against you". This 16-year-old guy sitting toward the back muttered to himself (out loud), "I'd be stuffed!"

Now, that's not a very profound way of putting it, but personally I agree with him.

I don't know anyone who would want their actions, words or thoughts shown to others, let alone to God. I suspect the editors of *Cleo* may even begin to believe in guilt if they knew their films were going to get a showing with the Almighty himself.

The reality is, despite all the noises to the contrary, we are moral beings. We are all wired to know the difference between right and wrong, even though our wiring gets a little crossed from time to time (I know mine does).

Rules, glorious rules!

It's impossible to talk about 'right' and 'wrong' without mentioning rules. But the problem is, rules are one of the things people like least about religion. I wish I had a dollar for every person I've spoken with who's said, "Yeah, I like Christianity and all that but I can't stand the rules. I'd go crazy trying to keep all those commandments."

This may come as a surprise to you, but I've got to admit I love God's rules. I think they're just fantastic. In fact, I can't get enough of them. Give me rules! Let me explain before you think I am totally weird.

God's rules are a lot like the rules of your favourite sport—they are not there to ruin the game but to make the most of the game. Rules in sport are what gives each game its character, they protect players from unnecessary injury, and they enhance the players' performance. For instance, I'm glad that Rugby Union has an *unlimited tackle rule*. In my opinion it makes Union a much more flowing game to play and to watch than League. I'm glad that League has a *no head high tackle rule*. It's this rule that keeps these giants from breaking their necks more often than they already do. Then there's soccer—my favourite game. The *offside rule* in soccer enhances the play of both team and individual. It means instead of just belting the ball from end to end, the team has to move it strategically up through the multi-talented midfield, to the brilliant strikers, and into the back of the net.

Like I said, give me rules

God's rules about life are just the same, but even better. God's commandments are about the best life. They are there to give life its dynamic character. They are there to protect us from getting unnecessarily hurt. And they certainly enhance our performance as players in God's world. Take God's rules about sex for example. As I said in the first chapter, God's commandments about sexuality are there to protect us from the shallow experience offered by the world's 'sexperts', and to give us sexual enjoyment in the context of lifelong trust and companionship. Take God's rules about beauty and image. God insists that we don't get caught up in the obsession to look beautiful, not because he is against beauty, but because he wants to protect us from the self-esteem problems associated with never measuring up. He also wants us to grow in 'inside' beauty, so that we can have a proper perspective on life. God's rules are good.

And so it is appropriate that we feel guilt when we go against God's wishes. Guilt is not an unnecessary feeling at all. It is often a very good reminder that there is a better way to act. More importantly, it's a good reminder that we should ask the Creator for forgiveness. Our defiance of his wishes is unacceptable. And the reality is, he does see everything—just like it was in a film. But the great news that Jesus came to bring to the world was that, despite our failure to recognise God's authority as Creator of this world, he still holds out an offer of forgiveness. Put another way, despite the bad bits in the films of our lives, God is willing to accept us and even direct a new film for us.

For suspicious minds

1. Have you done things that you are ashamed of?
2. How do you think you would go if God viewed the movie of your life?
3. Do you think rules are good things or bad things?

4

The surprise of my life

PURSUING THE HUNCH

In Year 9, my friends and I were the class clowns. We never burnt the school down or anything, but it seemed like hardly a day went by without one of us getting busted for something. Actually, I remember one teacher whom we gave a particularly hard time. His name was 'The Nose', because he had a huge one.

One day, a friend, Ben, and I bought a packet of party-poppers from the newsagent across the road from school.

Actually, I'm not so sure that we bought them. Anyhow, these were the kind where you pull the string and streamers explode out of the small plastic bottle. We got to Geography early that morning and taped one popper to each leg of The Nose's desk. We tied fishing line to the strings and wound it to the back of the classroom where we sat down. The class filed in and so did the teacher. Half way through the lesson, when all was quiet and the teacher was at his desk, we counted to three and pulled the line. It was loud. Streamers took off in all directions. One almost went up The Nose's nose (a large target). Ben and I quickly threw the fishing line to two (not very bright) girls next to us, so they would get into trouble. We got caught though, because we were laughing the most.

If you had asked me in Year 9 to name two things I thought I would never do or become, my answer would have been simple:

1) a musician

2) a Christian.

The closest I had come to being a musician was making it into the primary school choir. I remember there was only one lunch time to audition all the singers and I was near the back of the queue. The bell went before they had a chance to test my voice, so they kindly accepted me anyhow. Unfortunately, during the first rehearsal I got kicked out for mucking up.

The closest I'd got to religion before about age 15 was attending a funeral. I had never gone to church or Sunday School and no-one in my family showed the least bit of interest in religious stuff.

Turning out as a musician surprised me. Turning out as a Christian surprised everyone. Although I had a sneaking suspicion that Christians were on to something, I never dreamed of getting close enough to find out what it was. My introduction to the Christian faith was full of surprises.

The first startling discovery I made was that you could be normal and Christian at the same time. Like most Australians, I was sure 'getting religious' involved wearing sandals over your socks, pulling your jeans (or slacks) up under your arms, eating all your vegetables and going to bed by nine. Christianity and the 'dag' seemed to be closely related.

It's easy to understand why this is the common view. TV often portrays religious people as old-fashioned dags— usually, an old, senile minister who always says a lot but never anything meaningful. Or, take *The Simpsons*. I love that show but its portrayal of the Flanders family—narrow-minded, overly joyful, sickeningly 'nice'—doesn't do much for people's image of Christians. The Rev Lovejoy is slightly better but his sermons are pretty blah, blah, blah—boring. I don't think the TV stations have got it in for Christians, but the image of the 'religious loser' is used so often that people start to believe it.

The Hollywood Jesus films shown around the time of Easter don't help either. Have you seen one? The Jesus character nearly always has pretty, long, blonde hair, blue eyes and dresses up in a long white nightie. Basically, he's a wimp. Who'd want to side with him? *The Passion of the Christ* by Mel Gibson goes part of the way to redressing the wimpy Jesus but the film is so shocking I'm not sure Mel's Jesus provides an image that many of us want to hold in mind.

Toward the end of Year 9, my Scripture class got a new teacher. This lady was a normal, middle-aged mum from down the road who would come and teach us about God and stuff. She was normal and Christian at the same time. I'd never met one of those.

None of us could figure this lady out. Why would a nice, seemingly sensible person like her volunteer to teach a class like ours? It was this teacher who changed my mind about what religious people are like.

One day, she invited our class to her house on Friday afternoon for Bible study and scones. Obviously, the idea of Bible study didn't excite us, but my mates and I thought we'd test her out on those scones. We turned up one Friday and, sure enough, she'd prepared mountains of food which we quickly demolished. After eating, she got out her Bible. I thought, "Oh, oh. Here we go. Bible bashing time." To my surprise, she didn't preach at us. She just asked if we had questions about God and things. Boy, did we have questions and, one by one, she answered them from the Bible.

I distinctly remember one question that I asked her when none of my mates were around. It went something like this: "If God was true—which he's not of course—what would he think of my life?"

The answer to that question was the most startling discovery of my life. I learnt that God really cared for me. Now don't get me wrong. I do not mean a soppy type of caring. (It's easy for blokes to hear that God loves them and think, "Er, yuck!") I'm talking about the kind of love that sees us as we are—the good, the bad and the ugly—and still cares. It's a gutsy kind of love.

Up until that point, I guess I'd thought of God as a kind of grumpy bearded fellow who loved throwing lightning bolts at bad people. If he ever smiled, it was only when people were good and went to church. Or so I thought.

I knew I wasn't one of the good people who went to church but nor was I really bad. I never did drugs or stole cars. I was just a selfish, 15-year-old jerk.

After school I used to shoplift a fair bit. Usually, it was just a few Mars Bars down the pants. Only occasionally would I steal more serious things. Then, in the late afternoon, I'd often head down to the house of a friend who lived right next to Taronga Zoo. Countless times, we jumped the quarantine fence, ran through a bit of bush around the koala cage and spent an hour walking through the zoo annoying the animals and keeping clear of the officials. Looking back, I was a bit stupid breaking in. I was actually a zoo club member and could get in free anyhow.

For about five years, I learnt martial arts—that's the art of hurting people really well. I was right into it. I woke up before 6 am every morning to train, train, train. Then I'd go to school and find people to practise on. It was my life. I didn't get into many serious fights at all. But hurting just a couple of people is enough to get confidence, a big head and a reputation.

I didn't exactly feel guilty for all this stuff, but I was pretty sure God wouldn't like me because of it. I was wrong.

It was right at this point that I met the Scripture teacher and heard about a God who still loved me and who didn't want to hold my wrongs against me. I didn't have an instant 'conversion', but over a period of a few months I found myself drawn to the God who loved me.

Finding out that I could be normal and Christian at the same time was fascinating. Learning that God could accept me—regardless of how I'd messed up—was amazing. But there was one more surprise to top it all off. God didn't just forgive me. It seemed as though he was actively helping me to change my life.

A little while before this, my mum took me to a child psychologist to see if they could help me change. I actually enjoyed these sessions, because I got to talk for a whole hour about my favourite subject—me. The psychologist suggested that losing my dad in a plane crash at age 9 might be causing my violent, 'anti-social' behaviour, but she offered no real solution. I also had allergy tests, where we discovered that I might be allergic to cow's milk. In an effort to make some change for the better, I was taken off all dairy products for several months.

No change.

However, once my friendship with God took off, there was a noticeable difference. It wasn't a rapid change, but it was a major one.

From my point of view (and some of my friends as well) the most significant change was my temper. The fiery, violent aggression was stamped out. Now, don't misunderstand me. I'm not saying that I was once bad and now I'm an angel (my wife or mum will quickly correct you on that one). The point is that I've changed direction. I was once a selfish jerk, with my back turned to kindness, generosity, courtesy and sympathy. I had very little interest in putting other people before myself. Nowadays, I still frequently act like a fool, but I'm running toward those things I used to turn my back on. God is slowly changing my attitude. I read about Jesus in the Bible and think: "I want to be like that". I see his strength of character, his humility, his genuine interest in others and the way he stood up for people and I find myself praying: "Jesus, help me to be less of a jerk and more like you".

For me, being a Christian has been full of surprises. What began as a sneaking suspicion has blown into a huge reality. Like most Aussies, I had a hunch there was something more to life than beer and footy. I also had a hunch that the 'something more' could be found by looking into Jesus. When I decided to go with my hunch, I discovered more than I ever bargained for.

For suspicious minds

1. What sort of mental picture do you currently have of:
   - God
   - Jesus
   - Christians in general?

   Are these pictures fair do you think? What are they based on?
2. What's your hunch about God and Christianity? Do you think there might be something to it?

PART 2

some nagging
doubts

5

Science vs. God

BUT DIDN'T SCIENCE GET RID OF GOD?

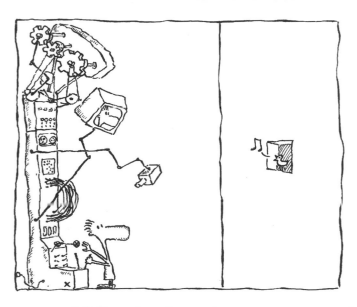

In many high schools and universities today, it is common to hear people say that science has somehow disproved God or at least made God irrelevant. This is not a new suggestion, but it's one that troubles some people. It may surprise you to know that until recently, theology ('the study of God') was known as the 'queen of the sciences'. Tell that to your biology teacher/lecturer and he or she will probably laugh at you and say, "Thank God we know better now!"

Little do we realise, though, that the debate between science and religion has more to do with attitude than with evidence. Religious people are often paranoid about being hit over the head with the latest theory against God (soon to be replaced with another one, of course) and many so-called 'scientific' people are equally paranoid and suspicious about anything that can't be analysed in a laboratory.

I want to talk about this issue in three stages, like three rounds of a boxing match. Firstly, I'll try to explain how people came to see science in opposition to belief in God. Then I'd like to show how modern scientists are thinking again about the possibility of God. And thirdly, I want to show that the highly billed 'Science vs. God' bout is really a big non-event!

Round 1: The deposed queen

What started this separation between the queen of the sciences and the rest of science? Without wanting to be too simplistic, let me describe some key events in this process.

In high school, we are taught that the earth and the rest of the planets revolve around the sun. But people haven't always thought this. In fact, before the 16th century, everyone was taught (by scientists) that the earth was the true centre of the universe. Around that time, an astronomer, mathematician and physicist named Galileo argued that the earth was not the thing around which everything else revolved. The established church of Galileo's day, on the recommendation of their scientific advisers, did not appreciate his ideas at all. They insisted that the earth was the centre of the universe. Unfortunately, the church also claimed that this was what the Bible taught on the issue—even though the Bible says no such thing. Poor Galileo got into a lot of trouble for his views and was forced to publicly deny his theories. Of course, we now know that he was mostly right, and the church was mostly wrong.

Critics of the church have not allowed her to forget this blunder. Slowly but surely, Christianity has been pushed out of the sphere of academic credibility. This Galileo incident symbolises the beginning of the 'Science vs. God' mentality.

The famous scientist, Charles Darwin, entered the Science vs. God bout when, in 1859, he proposed his theory of evolution by natural selection. We have all had to think about evolution at school—it was the topic of debate that made Year 10 science lessons bearable. To jolt your memory, Darwin suggested the principle of the survival of the fittest. Those animals which had characteristics which allowed them to adapt to their environment were most likely to live long enough to reproduce and pass on those 'survival characteristics' to the next generation. Darwin supposed that if this process occurred over millions of years, it might account for the many different species found on the earth. They could have all developed from the one starting point.

As you can imagine, the atheists (people who believe there is no God) were very pleased. Finally, they had a 'scientific' theory that explained our world without the influence of a Creator. All living things, including humans, could have simply evolved from the same 'primordial soup', as it has been called. This and various other factors further widened the gap between science and faith in God.

As an aside, it is interesting that Darwin himself believed in God and didn't view his theories as a threat to belief in God (at least not until later in his life). In fact, in his book, *The*

Origin of Species, there is a reference to God as the Creator who "originally breathed life with its several powers into a few forms or into one". In his later years, Charles Darwin commented:

> I was a young man with unformed ideas. I threw out (to people) guesses, suggestions, wondering all the time over everything; and to my astonishment the ideas took like wildfire. People made a religion of them.

Darwin's ideas were taken on like an alternative religion by many people. They reasoned that if nature, not God, was the ruling force behind our past and our future, we might as well forget about religion. If there's no God and we are just an interesting mutation in the ape kingdom, then let's live like we believe it! A philosopher named Friedrich Nietzsche rose to prominence during the time of Darwin. He popularised the phrase 'God is dead' and encouraged a new way of living that excluded morals and religion. Science and philosophy were now joining together in their dismissal of faith in God. Round one was a resounding victory, it seemed, to science.

Round 2: God back in the ring

It's no wonder that modern society has progressively considered devotion to God as a way of committing intellectual suicide. Many people feel that when Christians go to church they must leave their brains at the door and pick them up after the service. Such a view, however, is rapidly losing credibility as more and more of the great minds of our century are turning to God for a satisfactory answer to the big questions raised by science.

21 C magazine ran an article entitled 'God and science'. It discussed an interesting shift in modern scientific thinking.

> One of the reasons why physics has become so appealing to a

wider public is precisely because its theories are now giving us a picture of a universe that apparently has the stamp of a higher creative power on it.

John Polkinghorne, President of Queens' College at Cambridge University and one of the leading high-energy physicists of the last 30 years, said this about the origin of the universe:

There is no free lunch. Somebody has to pay, and only God has the resources to put in what was needed to get what we've got.

A recent survey of professional scientists in the US found that when you compare the scientific academic community with the general American population there is no difference at all in the levels of church attendance or belief in God. In other words, it is simply not true to suggest that scientific knowledge somehow undermines faith in the Creator.

Closer to home, Professor Paul Davies, from the Australian Centre for Astrobiology, would certainly not claim to be a Christian but he is strongly convinced that the nature of the universe can only be explained by the existence of a supreme Intelligence—God. In fact, he has written books with such titles as *God and the New Physics* and *The Mind of God.*

Robert Jastrow is the former director of NASA's Goddard Institute for Space Studies. He describes how scientists are beginning to realise that the old 'queen of the sciences' may still be worth listening to.

The details differ, but the essential elements in the astronomical and biblical accounts of Genesis are the same ...

This is an exceedingly strange development, unexpected by all but the theologians. They have always believed the word of the Bible. But we scientists did not expect to find evidence for an abrupt beginning ...

> At this moment it seems as though science will never be able
> to raise the curtain on the mystery of creation. For the scientist
> the story ends like a bad dream. He has scaled the mountains of
> ignorance; he is about to conquer the highest peak; as he pulls
> himself over the final rock, he is greeted by a band of theologians
> who have been sitting there for centuries.

Jastrow is saying that many scientists are being forced to face the conclusion that what Christians have been saying for centuries does in fact fit the big scientific picture of the universe.

Of course, these are only a few examples of what some modern scientists think. None of what I have quoted proves that God exists or doesn't exist. But I have tried to show that believing in God is not unscientific or unintelligent and it is no longer considered foolish by the scientific community at large. Science gives us no reason to feel embarrassed about believing in God.

Round 3: The bout is called off

I hear some people argue, "I won't believe until there is scientific evidence that God exists". But think about the assumption behind this complaint. It assumes that for anything to be true it must be proved scientifically. If we really took this seriously it would be absurd. Can science prove or disprove that the 'Mona Lisa' was painted by Leonardo De Vinci? Can it prove or disprove that Jennifer Hawkins (Miss Universe 2004) is an attractive woman and U2 a great band? Can scientific analysis prove or disprove that I love my wife? The answer, quite simply, is no. And yet these are all things most accept as true—particularly the last one, for me.

There are things in life that are simply outside the sphere of science. We must remember that science does not hold a monopoly on 'truth' and does not have all the answers. In fact, while science is brilliant in some areas of study, it has absolutely no significance in others. It's not that science is inadequate; it is simply inappropriate. Science can only answer certain kinds of questions.

If you ask how something happened, science is usually pretty good at coming up with a theory (like evolution by natural selection for example). However, when you ask the question "Why?", the scientist is less comfortable. An illustration may help.

A young boy walks into the kitchen one morning to find a kettle boiling on the stove. Wondering why it is boiling, he asks his dad (who just happens to be a scientist). His dad promptly replies, "Well son, it's because the combustion of the gas transfers heat to the bottom of the kettle which, being a good conductor, transfers heat to the water. The molecules of water become more and more agitated, give off steam and there is your boiling." A little dissatisfied by his father's reply, the kid asks his mum the same question, "Mum, why is the kettle boiling?" Finally, he gets the answer he has been looking for: "The kettle's boiling because I'm about to make us all a cup of coffee".

The father explained how the kettle was boiling. The mum answered why. Similarly, science is great at speculating about the big how of the universe, but we must turn elsewhere to find out why.

Why does the universe work so intricately?

Why are we humans here?

Why do we feel a deep need to know the answers to such questions?

These and many more questions like them have troubled humanity since the beginning of time. Science will never answer these great queries about the meaning of life, nor does it even attempt to. We live in the most scientifically advanced age and yet people are still longing for answers. The more we find out about ourselves and the universe, the more we are realising how much we don't know. For every new discovery, a hundred new questions are raised.

Aldous Huxley, the author of *Brave New World*, was himself a renowned atheist. But even he saw the limitations of science:

> Science has 'explained nothing'; the more we know, the more fantastic the world becomes, and the profounder the surrounding darkness.
>
> The bout between science and God is called off due to the fact that the competitors were competing for different titles.

Tell me why

If our only explanation of life comes from science, what are we left with?

- Our origin—we are mutated flukes of evolution.
- Our life—we are each a collection of minerals and chemicals worth about $5.
- Our destiny—we will eventually rot and become food for worms.

If we let science try to explain the 'why' of life, this is what we are left with. Is this all there is?

I have a hunch that this kind of attitude causes despair for many people. We've been told the 'how' of life but not the 'why'. Finding out how we got here is fascinating—I could almost say that I enjoyed biology at school. But knowing why we are here is not only fascinating—it's crucial for our fulfilment and happiness.

Wanting to know the meaning and purpose of our lives

on this planet is sometimes looked at as being corny or old-fashioned, but experience shows that the human heart is never satisfied with the 'what' and 'how' of life. We have always cried, "There must be something more ..." Someone once said,

> There is a God-shaped hole in the heart of every person, and only God can fill it.

It is this same sense of meaninglessness and a longing for *more* that dragged one of my close friends down to the point where suicide seemed the only option. Here's part of a note my friend wrote to explain these feelings:

> I wish I could escape my life. I wish I could die. I feel lost in a world where no-one knows me as I really am. There is nothing in my life worth living for. I see no other way of ending the way I feel. I have no reason to hate my life but no reason not to. If only I could find someone to save me from myself.

Now, I know that most of us do not feel as empty or helpless as my friend. The average Australian still has a 'she'll be right' view of life. But I think it is also true that most of us would really appreciate a few answers to some of the deeper questions of life, questions that science does not ask and cannot answer.

The designer's purpose

Suppose we sent back in time (say, 150 years) the latest home theatre/entertainment system with Dolby Digital surround sound speakers, 5 disc CD/DVD changer, DTS decoder and 220 watt subwoofer. After getting over the initial shock, the scientists back then would have a great time analyzing the system. They would be amazed with the intricate components and design. However, 150 years ago they didn't have anything like a sound system. Recording technology was more an idea than a reality. The scientists would most likely begin by asking questions about how it works. The more important questions, though, would be: What does it do? What is its purpose? Why was such a thing designed in the first place? Meaning and purpose are more important things to know than structure and design, but these are the very things that the scientists might miss.

Imagine if the designer of the sound system also went back in time and explained the purpose of the unit. Many, many things would fall into place. It would then begin to make sense in the scientists' minds. Only the designer of the system could give them the whole picture.

I'm sure you can see what I'm getting at. Science is a fantastic field of knowledge. Lives have been saved, people have been entertained, moons have been walked on—all because of the brilliant discoveries of science. However, we must not forget that while we have advanced in technology, other areas of life have made no progress to speak about. We are the most entertained people in history but also the most bored. We are the most educated people but our wars are even more deadly. We know more but believe in less. We can communicate by satellite instantly with anywhere in the world but we are failing to communicate across the kitchen table (remember, over 100 Australian families are breaking up every day). Of course, this is not the fault of science. In most cases it's our fault. However, the more we neglect the 'spiritual' dimension to the big questions of life the more I think we're going to be let down, frustrated, and in some cases despairing.

What we need is to know the Designer's purpose. That is the missing link.

As singer, songwriter and now politician Peter Garrett has said, "We need a place we can draw the fabric of values from".

Something that "gives us a purpose, a hope, the ability to go on".

The Christian faith claims to offer that 'purpose'. It claims that the great Designer himself has entered our world in the person of Jesus Christ and revealed to us the answer to the big why questions about our life and the universe.

The purpose of the universe is not simply to function. The purpose of humanity is not merely to survive by feeding the various organs that operate the body. Just as the sound system is designed for a reason—to play good loud music—we too have a 'higher purpose'. I hope the rest of this book will make clear what our higher purpose is.

For suspicious minds

1. Have you come across the idea that 'science has disproved God'? Where did you hear it? What actual evidence was given?
2. What things make you doubt that God is there?
3. What things make you suspect that God really is there?

6

Bible myths

HOW CAN I TRUST THE BIBLE?

Actress Winona Ryder was recently reported as saying, "Religion is fiction. I've read the Bible. It's a great book, but it's a novel."

I'm sure Miss Ryder's opinion is shared by many others. In fact, probably the most common view of the Bible is just that—it's a book you respect but don't trust.

If you'd asked me at 15 what I thought of the Bible I would have answered, "It's irrelevant. It's historically unreliable. And on top of that, it's been changed through the years so you don't know what it originally said anyhow." Amazing isn't it? I had never actually read the Bible, didn't know the tests for historical reliability and couldn't tell you what languages it had been translated from, but I would still have given such a confident reply!

Many people warn us not to believe the 'myths' in the Bible. The funny thing is, the real myths are the ones *about* the Bible, not *in* it.

It's been 'lost' in the translation

How many times have you heard the following argument?

> The Bible was translated from one language to another, then into another and so on and on. By the time it got to our English, its original meaning was lost.

This is the 'Chinese whispers' effect: someone says something, you pass it on, someone else passes it on, and so on. By the time the last person hears about it, the original message has undergone several transformations. Has this happened to the Bible?

The fact of the matter is that most Bibles available today are taken directly from the original languages—Hebrew, Aramaic and Greek. Our knowledge of these languages is getting more and more precise which means that translations are actually getting more accurate, not less.

The argument about 'losing it' in the translation process really is a myth.

It's been changed

Then of course, some people argue that the scribes (those who copied and passed on the ancient Bible documents) decided to change the stories to suit themselves. An example of this argument might speculate that the famous walking-on-water story in the gospel of Mark, chapter 6, originally read something like:

> Not long before morning, Jesus came toward them. He was swimming in the water and was about to pass the boat.

Then (according to this argument) some ancient scribe thought to himself, "That's a bit boring. I know, I'll put some life into it." So now Mark 6:48 reads:

> Not long before morning, Jesus came toward them, He was walking on the water and was about to pass the boat.

The problem with this view is the *evidence*—there isn't any. You see, we have in our possession hundreds of ancient copies of the gospel of Mark (for example), found in many different places all over the ancient world. Let's suppose for a minute one adventurous scribe from Athens did decide to change Jesus' swimming into walking on water. Surely you would still expect to find the original swimming story in one of the many other copies we've uncovered. It's not as if the Athenian scribe could fax his changes through to his friends in Jerusalem, Rome and Corinth and get them to make the changes too. The fact is, of all the ancient copies of Mark, only one version of this story exists and it says Jesus walked on water.

This is just one example. However, the same principle can be applied to any Bible story. Without any evidence of what a scribe is supposed to have deliberately changed, it makes no sense to argue that he did so. Such a speculation is based on bias rather than evidence.

Then there is the issue of *motive*. Remember, it's not as if these scribes thought they were making copies of *Dolly* or *Cleo*, where if you make a change here and there it's not such a big deal. Scribes actually thought they were dealing with God's word. That's a hard concept for us to get our brains around but they really believed it. For these people, any change was a horrible crime against God. Put yourself in their shoes (sandals)—would you make changes?

It contains accidental mistakes

Others argue:

> OK! So maybe the scribes didn't make deliberate changes, but what about mistakes? What if, over the years, errors were accidentally over-looked? Surely that would make the Bible unreliable today.

The fact is, mistakes *were* made in some of the ancient copies of the Bible. Actually, I'm happy to share one with you.

The Gospel of Luke, chapter 8, verse 43, describes a woman who came to Jesus for healing:

> And a woman was there who had been subject to bleeding for twelve years [and she had spent all she had on doctors], but no-one could heal her.

So what? The problem is, the bracketed part of the above sentence appears in *some* ancient copies of Luke's Gospel (remember: we've found heaps) but not in others. Obviously, some scribe, somewhere, messed up, either including or excluding those nine words (actually, just five in Greek). As a result, scholars search through the many ancient copies of Luke to find out which is the most likely form of the original sentence.

Their conclusion determines how the sentence appears in our modern translations of the Bible. Often, as in the case of Luke 8:43, there will be a footnote in our Bibles telling us about the alternative form of the sentence.

Of course, this isn't the only 'mistake' in the ancient copies of the Bible but the others do not change the overall meaning of any Bible story or text.

Basically, what I'm saying is this. The people who made their living as scribes, despite errors like this, were extremely professional people. I'll try and illustrate just how skilled they were.

Suppose you sat down tonight and wrote out a copy of this whole book. Suppose 20 years later (when you're worried the ink may fade), your son makes a copy of your copy. Now his copy becomes the basis of the next copy 20 years after that. Imagine this process takes place every 20 years for the next 1000 years (that's 50 copies later). Now imagine it's the year 3000 and a debate flares up about whether you can trust the modern copy of *A Sneaking Suspicion*. What would it take to show that changes had not taken place over the 1000 years?

What if an ancient copy was discovered? What if archaeologists, digging the ruins of your house, found a large section of the copy you had made 1000 years before? Surely, if they found this and then compared it to the modern copy they would discover what sort of changes had taken place.

Well, by an amazing stroke of luck, a similar thing actually did happen with a large section of the Bible.

In the Spring of 1947, an Arab shepherd boy was searching for one of his goats among the valleys near the Dead Sea. Along the way he threw a rock into a hillside cave and heard the sound of breaking pottery. He climbed in to investigate, and found pottery jars containing leather scrolls wrapped in linen. These leather scrolls (called the Dead Sea Scrolls) turned out to be one of the most significant discoveries of modern archaeology. Among them were large sections of the Bible dated at about 2000 years old.

When these sections were compared with modern Bibles, the accuracy was astounding. What we read now, is in fact, what was written thousands of years ago. The ancient scribes did their job very well.

Anyone who argues that mistakes were overlooked in the copying process, and that this makes the Bible unreliable, probably needs to think again.

Telling the truth

OK! Let's suppose that nothing was lost in the translation process. Let's suppose the scribes didn't make deliberate changes. Let's even suppose the scribes made no significant accidental errors. That still leaves one huge question unanswered. How do we know the original authors were telling the truth in the first place? Maybe the Bible is simply a well preserved lie.

In previous chapters I've often referred to things Jesus is meant to have said or done. If Jesus never actually did these things, Christianity is nothing but a sick joke. So then, the records of Jesus' life, death, and resurrection (called Gospels) are a great starting point to show why I think the Bible writers actually told the truth.

The first thing to remember is that these four books are based on eyewitness accounts. Two of them (Luke and Mark) were written by men who personally knew or interviewed eye-witnesses. This would be like you interviewing me to write an essay on my wife, Buff. The other two (Matthew and John) may have even been written by eyewitnesses themselves (though in Matthew's case this is less probable): men who travelled and worked with Jesus for over three years. This would be like me writing an essay on Buff.

The second thing to keep in mind is that many of the eye-witnesses were either imprisoned or executed for proclaiming what they'd seen. You've got to ask yourself: If it was a lie and they knew it, why did they die for it? It's one thing to die for something you simply 'believe' in (heaps of people have done that) but it's another thing to die for something you actually know is false.

Imagine I came to you saying that I'd seen a UFO land in my backyard. Suppose it was illegal to make such claims and as a result I was thrown in prison until I retracted my statement. Add to this picture hundreds of other eyewitnesses, all claiming to have seen the same UFO, all thrown in prison, and after several months, all executed along with me, for our belief. What would you conclude?

At the very least, you would have to conclude that we all really believed a UFO landed in my backyard. The big problem you would then have is working out how on earth hundreds of normal, sane individuals came to believe they'd seen a UFO. Was it drugs? Was it an optical illusion? Whatever it was, it couldn't have been a lie.

When you come to the Gospels you have a similar problem, only bigger. What caused these people to really believe they'd seen Jesus teach, heal, die and then rise again? Could it have been a three-year long optical illusion? If they had simply made the whole thing up, why did they bother dying for a lie? Even those who weren't imprisoned or killed for their claims, still had to endure family ridicule, loss of jobs and many other forms of persecution.

It's almost embarrassing to think that I once so ignorantly dismissed the Gospels as mere stories. I realise now that nobody bothers dying for a fairytale.

We've looked at four of the most common myths about the Bible:

- Something was lost in the process of translating the Bible.
- The ancient scribes made deliberate changes.
- Accidental errors made by the scribes undo the Bible.
- The Bible is simply a well preserved lie.

As I said at the beginning, most of us have a hunch that the Bible is worth respecting but we have bought into the myth that it is also unreliable. My recommendation is to go with the hunch not the myth. Do something outrageous. Actually read it for yourself. The Gospel of Mark is a great place to begin. I think you'll find that the best argument for the Bible is the Bible itself.

For suspicious minds

1. What is your own view of the Bible? How have you come to this view?
2. Try reading the Gospel of Mark. Does it read like fiction to you?

7

The riddle of suffering

WHERE IS GOD WHEN IT HURTS?

During the Second World War, six million people (mainly Jews) were exterminated under Hitler's regime. Where was God when that happened?

In 1996, Martin Bryant went on a shooting spree at Port Arthur, massacring 35 people.

As I write this, millions of people are being displaced in Sudan. Many of these will die of starvation and disease. How can God allow it?

I hardly need to mention September 11, 2001, in New York, or October 12, 2002, in Bali. What was God doing?

In 1976, a plane took off from Bombay airport only to crash moments later, killing everyone on board, including my dad. If God's so caring, why didn't he do something?

For every tragic situation the same question can be asked: Why does God let people suffer so much pain?

I want to forewarn you, I don't think this chapter is going to be a completely satisfying solution. In fact, I don't think a perfect solution to this puzzle exists. The question we are looking at is not like asking, "What is two plus two?" This has an exact answer—"four". But there are some things in life which cannot be explained like this. For instance, if you asked me, "What exactly is love?", I'm not sure I could completely answer you. I can describe what love is like by giving you my impressions, but I can't immediately give you a complete answer. I can only point you in the direction of the answer. In a similar way, to solve the puzzle about suffering, I can only point you in a direction I think will make things a lot clearer.

Does suffering disprove God?

Over the years, I've heard a number of people argue that the fact that we suffer disproves the existence of God. The argument goes something like this:

> If God really knew everything, could do everything, and loved everyone, he would not only know about our suffering but he'd be able and willing to stop it. The fact that suffering does exist suggests that God does not.

This sounds reasonable at first, but actually the logic is not so water-tight. In fact, it is just as reasonable to argue that: 1) since God knows everything, we should accept that he has some grand reason, not understandable to our small brains, for allowing suffering to continue; 2) since God can do everything, he is more than able to achieve his 'grand' purpose; 3) since God loves everyone, his grand purpose must be a kind one and ultimately in our best interests. In other words, logically speaking, suffering does not disprove God's existence at all.

More than this, I can't help thinking that if there is no God, to ask questions about suffering is actually meaningless. Let me explain.

Take, for example, the terrible situation in Sudan where hundreds of thousands of people are on the brink of starvation as I write. Suppose for a minute that there is no God and that the universe is the result of a huge cosmic fluke. Suppose also that we humans evolved by chance through millions of years of evolution, during which the strong survived and the weak died out. If we really are just a mutated fluke, why should we worry about millions of our species dying out? If they are the weaker ones, why not allow nature to take its course and let them die? Why fight against the natural process of 'survival of the fittest'? If we are just advanced apes, why should we worry about the starvation of the weak, or the rape of the innocent? Such things happen in the animal world all the time and no-one gets upset. Faced with a great tragedy, few of us can resist the profound urge to ask, "Why?" or "How can this be?" However, if there is no God, everything that happens—good or bad—must be thought of as a result of the random, mindless wastage of evolution. All rapes, murders, famines and genocide, etc., are simply the outworking of 'natural selection'. To ask 'why' inside this view of the world, is not only meaningless, it's irrational. Such occurrences must be accepted as inevitable consequences of the natural order. In reality, however, nobody could follow this logic through. Such a view of the world is totally *unlivable.*

Even the most rampant atheistic professor of philosophy, if faced with the tragic rape or murder of his own daughter, will cry out *"Why?"*

Are we merely a fluke, a mutation, an advanced ape? If so, our questions about suffering are irrelevant. Suffering is natural and unstoppable. However, if there is a great Designer who values us, it makes sense to look at the pain and hardship in our world and ask "Why?"

Of course, I'm not saying that suffering proves there is a God. That would be silly. I am simply arguing that without God, questions about suffering are useless. In my opinion, anyone who thinks suffering disproves the existence of God would do well to think again. It seems to me that most people do have a sneaking suspicion that God is real, which leads them to wonder why our world is swollen with pain.

Does God hate us?

I'll never forget that night in a small country pub in NSW when I mentioned that God loved people. I was most of the way through a concert and I gave this short introduction to a song about God's concern for us. Out of the blue I heard a strained voice holler from up the back of the room, "How do you know God loves us when he takes people from our lives?"

I thought, "Uh oh", and tried to avoid a long conversation. We were in the middle of a rock 'n' roll show, but that wasn't going to get me off the hook. I saw the silhouette of a woman as she got up from her table and walked right up to the stage.

Again she pressed me, "How do you know God loves us when he takes people from our lives?" I told her I would love to speak with her after the show. She sat down and I went on with the show.

At the end of the night, I was packing up the equipment

when I caught her eye from up the back. She pointed at me and motioned with her finger to come and talk. I did. That night she told me her life story and it was a sad one. She had recently lost two of her closest family members in a car collision with a train. She was convinced that God had organized it to pay her back for her wrongdoing. She explained that she had betrayed her husband and gone off with another bloke who had since left her. She figured that God was so angry with her that he had decided to punish her by killing those close to her. I tried for some time to convince her that God was not how she imagined him, but she could not bring herself to believe it. As far as she was concerned, God hated her and that was it.

Was she right? Does God see our 'sinfulness' and inflict suffering on us as a kind of pay-back?

The Bible contains some pretty frightening stories about God's judgement. It seems that God occasionally does respond to human arrogance and evil by punishing people in some dramatic way. In one incident that comes to mind, God brought a sickness on the whole nation of Egypt because they were unjustly enslaving the Jews. God has occasionally acted in this way but this does not mean that all suffering is his direct punishment. In fact, people in Jesus' day had a habit of blaming hardship on the personal 'sin' of the sufferer. I know of at least three times that Jesus challenged this distorted view of God (e.g. in Luke 13:1-5). Jesus actually taught that God is not a spiteful God, out to punish our every wrong move.

Our freedom to choose

There is an aspect of human suffering that is often overlooked— our own will, our capacity to make decisions for ourselves.

It would have been very easy for God to have programmed all of us to be 'good'. He could have made us like robots so that we would never be selfish and never mess up. However, God did not want us to be merely obedient machines. He created us with a will so that we could relate to him, even though it causes him pain when we rebel against him.

If you knew that every time your girlfriend or boyfriend said they loved you it was only because they were programmed to do so, how would you feel? The valuable thing about love is that it is a choice. Someone has chosen to treat you as special. Sure, there are risks involved, but the value of someone choosing to love you outweighs the risk. Maybe this is what God had in mind when he gave us a will.

Imagine getting home tomorrow and finding your room filled with huge boxes. On each box is written 'Sony'. You start ripping open the boxes. Sure enough, inside you find the latest state of the art sound system—the one we sent back in time in chapter five. You take the instruction manual out of its packet but, due to excitement, you toss it aside and go it alone. You start attaching leads to the amplifier, connecting the various parts and place a speaker in each corner of your room for maximum effect. After an hour of work, it's looking good. Every lead has found a socket and every socket is full of one plug or another. You take out your favourite CD and place it in the player. You grab the remote control, count to three and press play.

BOOM!! The whole thing explodes into a million pieces. Your room fills with smoke and you are lying on the floor in a daze. Over in the corner is the unused instruction manual.

The point of this story is obvious: manufacturer's instructions are invaluable, but it's our choice to use them or not. The Great Manufacturer himself has also given us the freedom to choose. We can choose to live selfishly and destroy each other or choose to put each other first and get along. We can choose to love and respect God and find real life, or choose to ignore him and miss it.

It seems to me we too often choose to throw away the instructions and end up blowing the stereo to pieces. In Sudan, the government decided to spend money on military weapons instead of food. As a result, those dying of starvation in that country were left to rot. Much of the suffering in our world is a direct consequence of human selfishness and foolishness.

When I see around me rape, divorce, child abuse and starvation, I am strongly reminded of the huge cost of God giving us choices. Suffering does not please God. In many ways, it is the price he pays in allowing us to accept or reject his friendship.

Chaos

Our freedom to choose explains much of our suffering, but not all.

Why did my dad's plane blow up? Why did an earthquake take 100,000 lives in Armenia? Why did a flood destroy whole towns in India, leaving countless people dead or homeless? Surely these people didn't deserve it, and it certainly wasn't caused by anyone's choice. Is there an answer to this kind of 'natural suffering'?

Now, please understand that natural disasters are not a form of pay-back. Although the Hindu religion argues that the particular suffering of an individual is the direct result of their bad actions in this life or a previous one, the Bible teaches something very different. For example:

> I am sure that what we are suffering now cannot compare with
> the glory that will be shown to us. In fact, all creation is eagerly
> waiting for God to show who his children are. Meanwhile, creation

is confused, but not because it wants to be confused. God made it this way in the hope that creation would be set free from decay and would share in the glorious freedom of his children. We know that all creation is still groaning and in pain, like a woman about to give birth. (Romans 8:18-22)

Unless you have previously given this a bit of thought, that quote probably sounds quite weird. It says that the world is waiting, confused in its current state, decaying and in pain— even groaning to itself like a woman giving birth (believe me, that's serious!). In other words, it's in chaos.

According to the Bible, right at the beginning of things, God saw everything he had made and thought it was very good (see Genesis 1:31). So what went wrong to put it out of whack? We did. We humans fundamentally rejected God and decided to go it alone, to live life our own way. God's response to this was something like: "If you want to do it without me, then that is what you shall do. It will cost you your lives and it will pain me, but that is the choice you have made". The Bible says that when humans got out of step with God, right back at the beginning, it was not just men and women who were affected, but the whole world. God still keeps the world going. But things aren't as they should be, because we asked God to butt out. Death and decay have entered our world.

So what has this got to do with suffering? Very simply, some suffering is due to the universe itself being out of whack with its Creator. We're not told how this affects things like earthquakes and other natural disasters. We're simply told the universe is decaying, and that this is a terrible sign of an even more terrible fracture of relationship between our Creator and us. Thankfully, we're also told things will one day be restored— even recreated.

Things will get better

How's this for a description of God's future plan for the world?

> God will make his home among his people. He will wipe
> all tears from their eyes, and there will be no more death,
> suffering, crying, or pain. These things of the past are gone
> forever. (Revelation 21:3-4)

According to God's own book, there will come a time when he'll set things straight. Evil, selfishness, violence and deceit will be severely dealt with and removed from the planet. The things that cause us (and him) pain will be gone.

There's no doubting it—suffering has been a huge part of human history. Nearly all of us have felt deep pain at some time and others have endured it all their lives. However, after God judges the world things will change. There will be no barriers between God and his people, and the sorrow of this present world will be nothing but a dim memory. And it will be forever! I want to be there.

I'm longing for things to change, but that does not mean I can take my eyes off the present situation. Suffering is real right now, and although I find comfort in understanding God's future plan, I'm sure we can also find comfort 'here and now'. Let me try and explain.

God has suffered

At about 18, I began (again) to get confused and upset that God had let my father die. Even though I was a Christian and it was years since the plane crash, it started to overwhelm me. In such a situation, it's easy to find yourself asking God some pretty strong questions: "How can you understand my pain? What would you know about losing someone you love? When have you ever felt betrayed and rejected? When have you ever suffered?"

The most disturbing thing about these questions is that they have answers. If you start to read the Bible, it soon becomes clear that God could well ask us: "Who understands pain better than me? Who knows more about losing someone you love than me? Who has ever felt as betrayed and rejected as me? Tell me, who has suffered more than me?"

At the very centre of the Christian faith is the God who has suffered. Think for a moment about his story. He created the universe and made us the focus of his attention. However, we rejected him, and he suffered the loss of our friendship. To restore and rescue us, he sent his very own Son, who gave up his position of honour, glory and power and became a man—Jesus. He healed people, cared for them and offered his forgiveness. Eventually, people turned on him. Even his closest friends abandoned him. He ended up nailed to a cross, bleeding, suffering, dying for us all—even those who hated him. This is the God whom I had the arrogance to ask: "When have you ever suffered?"

If you were designing a God, would his pain, sorrow and rejection be part of the formula? If I were inventing a God, I'd make him the big success story. He'd come riding a Harley Davidson and everyone would think highly of him. However, this kind of God could not feel the pain of sick people. He couldn't cry with the girl who has been abused. He wouldn't feel sympathy for the bloke whose parents hate each other and take it out on him.

However, the God spoken of in the Bible does feel our pain. He can fully sympathise because he has greatly suffered.

Like I said at the beginning of this chapter, there is no simple, complete answer to the puzzle of human suffering.

Even if there was a logical explanation, I doubt it would comfort someone who is experiencing some personal tragedy. I mean, imagine trying to help my mum after losing my dad by saying, "Your husband died because of the bad karma of a past life and you are now suffering for the same reason". This may be an 'answer' (personally, I doubt it) but it is certainly not any comfort. The Christian faith is different. It does not offer one simple answer. Instead, it invites people into a relationship with the God who has suffered. He can bring comfort to the suffering person because he has been there first. In my mind this is far more satisfying than a quick, simple answer. Maybe God avoided revealing a full solution in the Bible because he wanted to comfort our pain, not just answer our questions.

For suspicious minds

1. Has the suffering of the world, or in your own life, ever made you doubt the existence of God?
2. How do you react to the arguments of this chapter about this?
3. Do you think God can sympathize with our suffering? Why/ why not?

God's elephant

WHAT ABOUT OTHER RELIGIONS?

Imagine that on your way home tomorrow you pass a circus where you see several blind-folded children climbing all over a huge elephant. One kid is hanging on to its tail. A couple have their arms around its legs. One is swinging on its trunk, and two or three are clutching the poor thing's ears. You get a little closer and discover they are having a fierce argument about what it is they have found. The one on the tail describes it as a kind of stringy rope. Those at the elephant's legs laugh at that explanation and insist it is more like a tree stump. Of course, the kid on the trunk says it's similar to a fire hose, and those clutching the ears think everyone else has gone mad because it is obviously far more like huge banana leaves.

The children hear you walking past and ask for your opinion. Let me suggest three different ways you could respond. Firstly, you could avoid their question by saying: "No comment, sorry. I steer clear of this kind of debate." Then again, you might accept all their opinions and reply: "Well, actually you are all correct in your own way". Thirdly, you may reject their views and state: "You are all wrong. None of you has the full picture."

This 'elephant story' and these three responses illustrate the ways many of us think about the different religions in the world.

Option 1: Avoid the issue

It really does appear that many religious people are climbing all over an elephant called God and arguing amongst themselves about what it is. The Buddhist says the way to 'enlightenment' is to follow Buddha's 'eight-fold path'. The Muslim disagrees, claiming that only strict obedience to Mohammed's teaching as found exclusively in the Koran will bring us Allah's (God's) favour. The Jew, of course, thinks they're all mad and argues that God has revealed himself only to the nation of Israel and to those who convert to Judaism. For those of us who are religious spectators, it all seems a bit odd.

All the confusion and arguing about religion just turns

some people off the whole subject. They say, "No, sorry. I avoid these kind of debates." On the surface, this makes some sense. But I can't help thinking that it's also a bit of a cop-out. The other day for instance, I was at lunch with my family and one of them said, "Religion is just like politics. It's simply one opinion against another. We should just avoid it." Avoiding a question is certainly an easy way out, but it never leads to answers. Of course, we all have a right to be uninterested in religion, but we should also realise that evading a question is not an answer in itself. I mean, lying on the beach thinking of calm waters does not solve the problem of an incoming 100-metre tidal wave! If the wave happens to be real, not just an idea or opinion, then it poses a slight problem.

However, if you've got this far in the book, it probably means you are more interested in answers than evasion.

Option 2: Accept every possibility

One possible answer to this question about the different religions is similar to the second response in the elephant story: "Well, actually you are all correct in your own way". For many of us, this seems the best solution. After all, saying all religions are true is a very tolerant and accepting way of looking at things. It also discourages the fierce arguments that so often occur.

For all its good points, this attitude has one big problem. It fails to recognize that most religions contradict each other. For instance, Hinduism teaches that there are millions of different gods in the universe, but Jews claim that there is only one. Now, I was never great at maths but even I can work out that 'millions' and 'one' are not the same idea. If there is only one God, there are not millions. If there are millions, there can't possibly be only one. Someone has to be wrong.

Again, Buddhism claims that everyone is reborn after death

to come back as another creature. This completely contradicts the teaching of Islam, which says that everyone lives and dies once. They can't both be true, can they?

It just doesn't make sense to say that all religions are true when they teach such different and contradictory things. If two people make two completely contradicting statements, we can't accept both, can we? Either one is right and the other wrong, or they are both wrong. For example, suppose you came over and had dinner with me and my wife and during the meal you asked if Buff was pregnant. If she answered 'no' at the same time that I said 'yes', you'd have a problem. (So would we!) To my knowledge, you can't be pregnant and not pregnant at the same time. So either I knew something she didn't, or she was right and I was mistaken. No-one in their right mind would accept both of our answers as true.

GK Chesterton—an old, smart, dead guy—once said:

An open mind should be like an open mouth. Its purpose is to chomp on something nourishing. Otherwise, it becomes like a sewer, accepting everything, rejecting nothing.

Sadly, some of us have fallen for the strange view that accepts all religions as true even though they contradict each other. Our minds become like a sewer—accepting everything, rejecting nothing.

Option 3: Reject every possibility

If avoiding the issue is no help and accepting all religions seems inadequate, maybe the third option is the best one—reject them all as false.

To many of us it seems arrogant to expect to know the answers to the really huge questions of life. I mean, how on earth can any single religion answer questions like: Who is

God? What is he or she like? Are there many gods or just one? How do you get to know this being or beings? Is there life after death?

What chance have we got of working out the solutions to these questions on our own? Because it seems so hard to find all the answers, many people decide just to reject all religions.

The photograph

Before we reject all faiths, however, I think there is one thing we should consider. We certainly don't need any more speculation about God and stuff, but what if we had a revelation? What if we were given information that we could never have discovered for ourselves? We may not be able to guess our way to God, but he could reveal himself to us. I'll explain what I mean.

Right now, try and guess what my wife looks like. I suppose you could make a few intelligent suggestions—she's a woman, she's probably in her 20s or 30s, and if you knew me, you could work out she would have to be a brunette! Beyond this, you would find it fairly difficult to come up with any clear, accurate description of Buff. However, if I gave you a photograph of her, you wouldn't need to speculate. The photo reveals her. This is what I mean by a 'revelation'—something which tells us about God so that we don't have to speculate.

The question then is, has God ever personally revealed himself? Where is his photo?

Mohammed, Buddha, Moses, Guru Nanak, Confucius and the other great founders of religions were undoubtedly amazing people. They had insight, leadership skills and brought inspiration to thousands of their followers. But none of them ever claimed to personally reveal God. None of them said "Look at me and you will see God". There is, however, one exception.

Now, before you say, "Of course you reckon that Jesus personally revealed God—you're a Christian!", let me make one thing clear. Some people think that Christians have to believe in Jesus because they're Christians. But that's like saying that doctors only believe in medicine because they're doctors. It's the other way round. Doctors become doctors because they are convinced about the value and effectiveness of medicine. In a similar way, I am a Christian because I was first convinced about Jesus. Let me get back to my point.

Probably the most outrageous claim Jesus made was that he was the 'photo' of God. One of his followers once asked him to reveal God to them. This was Jesus' reply:

> Philip, I have been with you for a long time. Don't you know who I am? If you have seen me, you have seen the Father. How can you ask me to show you the Father? Don't you believe that I am one with the Father and that the Father is one with me? (John 14:9-10)

Maybe Jesus was mad. Maybe he was an arrogant fraud. But maybe he was God's photo. I can't make you believe what I believe. I can only say that as I read the records of Jesus' life, teaching, death and resurrection, I am constantly forced to make a decision about this man. The only conclusion which seems to make sense is that Jesus was, and continues to be, God's supreme revelation—God in the flesh.

Personally, I can't bring myself to avoid, accept or reject all religions. If God has a photo (so to speak), I want to see it. I want to know him, respect him and do what pleases him.

At the beginning of this chapter, I asked you to imagine several blind children climbing over an elephant. The story is often told to argue that religion is simply a guessing game in which we all have our own opinion. However, although each child had an opinion, the fact of the matter still stands. It wasn't a rope, a tree trunk, a fire hose or a couple of banana leaves. It was an elephant. The real point of the story is easily overlooked. Regardless of what each child thought, truth was truth. It simply took a broader vision to see it. One person in the story actually saw things as they were. When the children asked for your opinion, would it have been arrogant to tell them what you saw?

Christians are often criticized for being arrogant and self-righteous and, unfortunately, they sometimes are. But in fact, Christians do not declare that they are completely right and everyone else completely wrong. They simply answer honestly about the way they see things. They've been shown God's photo. They have seen God's elephant. His name is Jesus.

For suspicious minds

1. From your own experience, and from this chapter, what do you think are the major differences between Christianity and other religions?
2. People sometimes challenge God by saying, "I'll never believe in God unless he actually comes down here and I see him with my own eyes". If Jesus is God's 'photo', has God already answered the challenge?
3. What do you currently think about Jesus?

9

Too good for God

WON'T GOD ACCEPT ME IF I'M GOOD ENOUGH?

Some years ago, I had a very interesting conversation with a young bloke who had come to see the band I used to sing for in a small NSW country town. He had with him a pile of university notes on philosophy and psychology, which one of his teachers had given him to read.

He'd heard me talk about my faith, so he wanted to know what I thought of the notes and whether or not they'd help clear some of his confusion about life.

Now, I've got nothing against philosophy or psychology, but I advised him to avoid them because I was worried he would end up more confused than he already was.

I invited him to come back later if he wanted to discuss it further. Sure enough, later that afternoon, as we were setting up for another concert, he came back. This time he had with him a large exercise book. What I read in it amazed me. On each page of the book he had ruled columns. Across the top he had written the days of the week. Down the side he had listed a dozen or so moral characteristics. Things like: patience, kindness, consideration, self-control. Then there was a score out of ten for every day next to each characteristic. He was grading himself. He explained that he was keeping a record of his life, to see if he was good enough for God to accept him.

Now, I don't know too many people who go to these kind of lengths to measure their life, but I do know lots who have a similar view about how to be accepted by God.

There is a great myth in our society which says that 'being good' is good enough for God. It's often expressed like this: "I'm a good person. I've never murdered anyone or done anything even remotely as bad. God will give me the nod." It's as if God has a huge set of scales with which he measures the good in our lives against the bad. If the scale weighs more heavily on the good, we're 'in'; if not, we're 'out'. If the Bible is anything to go by, this couldn't be further from the truth. Listen to this story that Jesus once told:

Two men went into the temple to pray. One was a Pharisee [these were the religious leaders of Jesus' time] and the other a tax collector [these guys had a reputation for ripping others off and were not liked]. The Pharisee stood over by himself and prayed, "God, I thank you that I am not greedy, dishonest, and unfaithful in marriage like other people. And I am really glad that I am not like that tax collector over there. I go without eating for two days a week, and I give you a tenth of all I earn."

The tax collector stood off at a distance and did not think he was good enough even to look up toward heaven. He was so sorry for what he had done that he pounded his chest and prayed, "God, have pity on me! I am such a sinner."

Then Jesus said, "When the two men went home, it was the tax collector and not the Pharisee who was pleasing to God".

(Luke 18:10-14)

I imagine that when Jesus told this story, it really offended some people. Imagine saying that the most religious person of the day was not pleasing to God and that God was on the side of a con-artist who simply apologised.

The Pharisee was a good, clean-living sort of a man. He wasn't greedy or dishonest and had a reasonably successful marriage as well. Who could ask for more? Why was Jesus so sure that God was displeased with him? The tax collector, on the other hand, was greedy and dishonest. People probably trusted him less than we trust our modern day used-car salesman. Why was Jesus so certain that God was pleased with this guy?

I think the issue Jesus is driving at is one of confidence. It isn't a matter of whose good deeds weigh most on the scales, but of where a person's confidence rests. It's obvious that the Pharisee thought highly of himself and just assumed that God would be on his side. This is an easy mistake to make. I have met heaps of people who think that being good is good enough. But the question could be asked: "Good enough by whose standard?" I mean, we may be able to live up to our own standards (since our standards are often determined by how we are already living). But what are God's standards?

According to the Bible, God's standards are a lot higher than ours. Do any of us really think we live up to them? Obviously, some people get closer than others, but no-one I've met even comes close. If none of us lives up to God's standards, how on earth can any of us be confident that he is happy with us?

Let me put it like this. Now, I'm a pretty good soccer player. In fact, I'm probably better than a lot of you readers (forgive me for the boasting). But if I met David Beckham, No. 23 for Real Madrid, or Wayne Rooney, the new sensation at Manchester United, I wouldn't even go near a ball. Compared to those guys, I am nothing of a soccer player. You see, it all depends on who you compare yourself to. You may well be a much nicer person than me, but I am a fairly low standard. Compared to God—that's the standard—even someone as nice as you does not measure up.

So you see, even though the Pharisee in Jesus' story was a 'better' person than the tax collector, he still had no reason to think that he was good enough, because compared to God's perfect standard even he looked pretty ordinary.

If none of us measures up to God's standards how can any of us become God's friends. Well, it certainly isn't by keeping a record of our good deeds, like my friend in the country town. We do it the way the tax collector did in Jesus' story. We place our confidence in God and his mercy, not ourselves and our 'goodness'. This is why the tax collector went home pleasing to God. He knew he couldn't meet God's standards. He knew he could never live up to God's standards, so he called on God to forgive him. He placed his confidence in a very kind God, who forgave him completely.

Meanwhile, the Pharisee was still trying to flex his 'moral muscles' and believe that he was good enough for God. Tragically, many people today are doing the same thing. Their confidence is in the wrong place—themselves and their own standards of goodness. According to Jesus, they too will never make it.

Now, of course, we're not meant to go around hating ourselves and having a low self-esteem. That's not Jesus' point at all. You can still have good self-esteem and be realistic about your failures. In fact, there are probably many more reasons to feel good about ourselves once we face the reality of our shortcomings and realise that, despite them, God still loves us and wants to forgive us.

The question must be asked: Am I trusting in my ability to please God or in his ability to forgive? Do I have a relationship with God based on humility, respect and love, or is it built on self-assurance? According to Jesus, the way we answer these questions will indicate whether or not we are God's friends.

At the beginning of the chapter, I told you about the young bloke who kept a record of his life in an exercise book. He later came to understand the same ideas that I have mentioned here and his response was amazing. When he discovered that being good is not good enough for God, he started to get excited. It dawned on him that trusting in his own moral achievement was actually getting in the way of a true friendship with God. He knew he could never meet God's standards anyhow. Like the tax collector, he asked God to forgive him and "went home pleasing to God". The huge smile on his face said it all. It was like someone had let him off a huge debt. Needless to say, he no longer needed or wanted that exercise book.

For suspicious minds

1. Try reading the story of the Pharisee and the tax collector in Luke, chapter 18, verses 9 to 14.
2. What is it about the Pharisee that God doesn't like?
3. Do you act towards God like the Pharisee, the tax collector or some other way?
4. Do you think anyone is good enough to please God?

PART 3

the guts of it all

10

The death factor

AFTER THE GRAVE, THEN WHAT?

It's the world's one unavoidable fact. And yet, it's also the world's most avoided topic of conversation. We often act as if it doesn't happen, but at the same time, most of us are aware that one out of one people die. 'You will die' is the most trustworthy prediction that anyone can make. The following poem makes this point very clear. It's called 'Death Lib' by Steve Turner.

The really wonderful thing about death
is that all major religions agree on it,
all beliefs take you there,
all philosophy bows before it,
all arguments end there.
Con men can't con it. Thieves can't nick it.
Bullies can't scare it. Magicians can't trick it.
Boxers can't punch it, nor critics dismiss it.
Don't knows can't not know. The lazy can't miss it.
Governments can't ban it, or the army defuse it.
Judges can't jail it. Lawyers can't sue it.
Scientists can't quell, nor can they disprove it.
Doctors can't cure it. Surgeons can't remove it.
Einstein can't halve it. Guevara can't free it.
The thing about dead—is we're all gonna be it.

I'd like to ask you a question. It's one of the very few questions that is relevant to everyone who has ever lived. What do you think will happen to you after you die?

In our world there are three common, but very different, answers to this question. In the next two chapters, I'd like to explain each of them with their pros and cons. You may be young, cool and happy with life and feel no need to think about such depressing stuff. But if you make it through the chapter, I hope you'll agree that death doesn't have to be as depressing as it sounds.

View 1: We simply rot

We've all heard people say, "When I die, I'll just rot". What they normally mean is that, when the machine in our chest stops pumping vital minerals, gases and nutrients to the rest of the organs in our body, the machine in our head will also stop. This will result in death. At this point, the five dollars worth of raw materials that make up our bodies will steadily decompose, eventually leaving a mound of dirt. This will rot and there's nothing more to say.

To be honest, I have two big problems with this explanation. Let me outline them for you.

It's based on a strange assumption

People who believe we simply rot usually base their belief on the strange assumption that science must prove something before it can be regarded as true. They argue that science can prove that we rot, therefore it's true. Then they add that because there is no scientific proof for life after death, it must be false.

Why do I think this a silly assumption?

As I pointed out in an earlier chapter, there are many aspects of everyday life that cannot be proved or disproved by science and yet are still true. Some things are just outside the field of scientific investigation. There is no scientific proof, for example, that Bob Dylan wrote 'All Along the Watchtower', or that Captain Cook ever set foot on Australian soil. Does this mean that these momentous events in human history never occurred? Of course not. They are simply 'truths' of a non-scientific nature.

Science is extremely valuable in some areas of life— medical, technological and environmental issues for instance. However, it is virtually irrelevant in others—art, relationships and personal happiness, for example. I would add 'life after death' to this second list.

I'm the first to admit there is no scientific evidence for life after death, but so what? It seems strange to me that we accept many things in life without scientific evidence and yet when it comes to life after death some people cry out, "Where's the evidence?"

There is also another reason for my scepticism.

It takes the value and purpose out of our lives

If we are worth only a few dollars at birth and end up as a few kilograms of dirt at death, what occurs in between has no real value or purpose. Our lives count for nothing. Think about it—if our bodies are just machines that work for 70 years and then break down only to rot, what's the point of life? I mean, you might as well shoot me, split the five bucks between my wife and kids, and make use of me as compost.

This sounds absurd doesn't it? It might even make you angry. How can I speak like this about human beings? Something inside us refuses to believe that we don't have value and that our lives are without purpose. However, if we are simply organisms that die and rot, it's hard to avoid the logical conclusion that life is pretty darn pointless. This is another reason why I don't buy the view that death is the end of it all.

A while ago, a scientist called Sir John Eckles was awarded a Nobel Prize for his research on the brain. He is no thickhead. He once made the following statement.

The brain is a machine that a ghost (or soul) operates.

If he is right and we are more than machines, then there is some hope, meaning and purpose to this life. Life suddenly takes on a new and wider dimension.

If death is not the end, what comes after?

View 2: We come back again

Reincarnation is the belief that every animal has a soul which leaves the body at death and is re-born into a new animal or person. The process is repeated again and again.

This view of death seems to be gaining acceptance in our country. In fact, I think it is probably more widely believed than the 'rot' idea. There are at least three factors that make reincarnation attractive. Firstly, it appears, on the surface, to explain what happens to the soul after death. Secondly, it gives us the hope that our own existence will continue. And thirdly, it is more comforting to believe that we come back in another form than it is to think that we die and then face some kind of assessment of our lives. Despite these apparent pluses, I wonder if reincarnation raises more questions than it answers. Here are a few of them.

Does it solve or create evil?

Central to the teaching of reincarnation is the law of 'karma'. Karma is thought to be the 'balancing out' rule of the universe. It is the way the universe corrects itself. Your 'karma' determines what form you take in your next life. For instance, if you've been bad in this life, you may come back as a wombat. If you're a woman and you've been good, in your next life you may come back as a bloke. (Sorry girls! Please don't get angry with me. This is strictly what reincarnation teaches.)

The law of karma not only determines what you come back as but also the circumstances of your next reincarnation. For example, if you murder someone in this life you may well be the victim of a murder (or equivalent evil) in your next. On the surface, this appears to have a nice balancing out effect. However, if it were true, it would actually create evil, not solve it. Let me explain.

Suppose you did commit a murder in this life and in your next reincarnation are the victim of some evil to balance it out. For that to happen, someone else must commit an evil against you, which then means the perpetrator of that evil must come back as the victim of some other evil, which means someone else must commit an evil against him, which means he must come back and be the victim of another evil, which means ...

You get my point, right? Your one murder begins a whole cycle of evil. Reincarnation doesn't solve evil at all.

Does it make sense?

In the days when I was a martial arts fan I spent a lot of time with a group of people who were right into reincarnation. I remember feeling very out of it because they all claimed to remember their past lives and I couldn't recall mine.

Do you have any recollection of your past lives? My guess is that you don't. If not, why not? It seems weird to me that the same soul gets reincarnated and yet can't remember what it was doing last time around. If we can't remember, what's the point of living so many times? Surely it would make more sense to recall our past and learn from it so as to build on our strengths and avoid our mistakes.

Reincarnation is meant to provide us with a cycle of birth and re-birth, leading us forward toward 'Nirvana' (not the rock band). Nirvana actually means to be 'blown out' like a candle (hence the rock band I guess!), but it is used to describe the state of perfection when we are at one with the universe and with God. If our world is the result of thousands of years of reincarnation, you would expect it to be getting better, wouldn't you? Is it?

Does it offer any hope?

The goal of life, according to reincarnation, is to work off bad karma by doing good deeds and climbing the ladder towards perfection. I don't know about you, but from what I see in my life—selfishness, pride, unkindness—I wonder if I am building bad karma rather than working it off.

If we build bad karma in this life we must live again and try to work it off, but in that life we are likely to build more bad karma because we already start it with black marks against our name. We get trapped in a vicious cycle where the bad just get badder.

Is there a way to escape this 'wheel of reincarnation'? Is there any hope?

The grave question

Recently, a family friend passed away with cancer. Before he died he started to 'become religious'. There are those who would be slightly cynical about this, but such cynicism is ridiculous. I mean, if you realise you're about to fail maths at school, you would be foolish not to take it more seriously and spend more time at your desk in preparation. If I owned a business that started to run out of money, I'd be a fool not to be more careful with my spending and make safety plans. Likewise, it makes perfect sense to me that when someone's life is running out, they think more carefully about death and make some safety plans.

Of course, you are probably like me—young, alive and planning to stay that way for some time. It's easy to feel invincible when you're young and healthy. Thinking about death can seem like an annoying interruption. I don't want to depress you and I certainly don't want to leave you scared, but let me repeat the question I asked at the beginning of the chapter.

What do you think will happen to you after you die?

Do you imagine you'll simply rot and nothing more, or do you believe you have a soul that will be reincarnated into another body?

Or do you, like me, feel that neither of these answers can solve the question of the grave? Well, there is another option.

For suspicious minds

1. What do you think will happen to you when you die? What evidence do you have to support your belief?
2. Think about the things you currently value most in your life—how does the reality of death affect the values of these things?

11

The life factor

THE EXPERT ON DEATH CAN TELL YOU ABOUT LIFE

When I was in year 10, a friend of mine named Robert was doing maths a few classrooms away. While they were waiting for the teacher to arrive, he and another mate, Andrew, thought they'd pass the time by having a play rumble. Andrew pushed Rob on the chest and he collapsed. Only a few of us knew that Rob had a heart condition. He died moments later.

If you've ever experienced something like this you'll understand the trauma. What made it even harder for us is that a couple of weeks before this, Robert, some mates and I spent a night camping together. That night, we talked for hours about what we thought of God, death, heaven and stuff like that. It never crossed any of our minds that a few weeks later one of us would know for sure.

Rob wasn't a 'religious' bloke by any stretch of the imagination, but from the things he said when we went camping together that night, he certainly had a hunch about God and stuff. He also knew quite a few Christians who'd tried their best to explain what it meant to know God. Who knows? Maybe Rob got his foot in the door at the right time.

Now please don't get me wrong. I'm not saying Christianity is simply an eternal-life insurance policy. I'd be short-changing Jesus if I made out that he only came to give us a free ticket to paradise. However, it is still true that while he walked the earth, Jesus did make many fascinating—even outrageous—claims about death and heaven and hell. Let's see what the Bible has to say on these all-important matters.

Whom can you trust?

The best summary I can find of what Jesus taught about death is found in Hebrews 9:27:

> We die only once, and then we are judged.

This statement flatly disagrees with the two views of death we have just discussed. If it is true, it contradicts the 'die and rot' idea. The statement also insists that "we die only once", so it is difficult to see how reincarnation fits in.

Of course, just because this statement was made doesn't mean it's true. It's not possible to prove any view of death.

You can only compare, discuss and then decide which view is the most reasonable. Before I go into detail about what Jesus taught, I want to explain why I think we should even bother listening to him.

Unlike the 'die and rot' or reincarnation ideas, what Jesus taught about death is not based on a strange assumption, does not take the value and purpose out of our life, and does not perpetuate evil. On top of this, it also seems to make sense and offer hope.

There is one extremely important reason why Jesus' teaching on death should be taken seriously. I'll explain.

Siddhartha Gautama, known as the Buddha, founded what is called Buddhism. He taught about death, and yet he was overcome by it. Mohammed founded the religion called Islam. He taught about death too, and of course it beat him as well. Then there was Bertrand Russell, one of the greatest atheists of the 20th century. He spoke and wrote about death and yet, sadly, he couldn't fight it off either. These were undoubtedly great men who have influenced millions of people throughout history. In fact, these men make The Beatles, U2 and Blink 182 look small-time. They had incredible brains, deep insight into life and an ability to sway people's thoughts that leaves our 'Coca-Cola' ads for dead (so to speak). There's one problem, though: they're all dead, so we have no way of knowing whether or not what they taught about death is reliable.

This is not the case with Jesus. Yes, he died, but one of the unique things about Christianity is that its founder died and then returned from the dead. This is not a fairytale but an event in history. I don't want to ridicule Mohammed and the Buddha or any other great religious teacher. I am simply pointing out that Jesus has one up on them all—he rose from the dead. (I'll say a lot more about Jesus' resurrection in chapter 14.)

If you need help understanding maths, who do you turn to? Your geography teacher? Probably not. Again, suppose you're keen to play the didgeridoo, who's most likely to give you valuable hints? Your local church minister? I think not. To learn about anything, it's best to seek the advice of an expert— in these cases, a maths teacher or an Aboriginal musician. Likewise, if you want to know about life after death, I guess you could ask a scientist or a philosopher, but it's probably a lot smarter to learn from someone who has experienced death and lived.

Jesus is the expert on the afterlife. The fact that Jesus died and rose again gives solid credibility to his teaching about death. This is extremely important to understand.

View 3

What did the expert himself teach? Jesus' view on death can be explained in three parts.

Be prepared, death can strike at any moment

A man once came to Jesus, complaining that he hadn't got his cut of his deceased father's money. Jesus knew this guy needed a change of perspective, so he told one of his illustrations to make a point. This is the story Jesus told:

> A rich man's farm produced a big crop, and he said to himself. "I'll tear down my barns and build bigger ones where I can store all my grain and other goods. Then I'll say to myself, 'You have stored up enough good things to last for years to come. Live it up! Eat, drink, and enjoy yourself.'"
>
> But God said to him, "You fool! Tonight you will die. Then who will get what you have stored up?" (Luke 12:16-20)

In Jesus' mind, we need to be prepared for death. The rich

man in Jesus' story had a 'Live it up!' attitude (sounds like he was an Australian). Jesus wasn't speaking against having fun in life, but he was warning us not to think we are invincible. He was also pointing out that we should care about the things that count—like God and life after death.

There is an ancient Middle Eastern legend I heard a while ago that makes the same point. I'll try to modernize it for you to make it clearer. The basic story is still the same.

A Sydney businessman once sent his secretary down to the shops to buy lunch. About an hour later the secretary ran back into his office white as a ghost and trembling with fear.

She said to her boss, "When I was down at the shops someone walked past and bumped into me. I turned to see who it was and recognized it was Death. He gave me a very threatening look. I dropped everything and ran straight back here. I'm sorry but I've got to get out of town and hide somewhere Death won't find me."

Her boss gave her some time off and she caught the next plane to Melbourne.

After work, the businessman was walking down the street when he noticed Death sitting in a cafe drinking a Coke. He went straight over and said to Death, "Why did you give my secretary such a threatening look at lunch time?"

Death replied, "That was not a threatening look; it was surprise. I was amazed to see her up here in Sydney because I have an appointment with her later tonight in Melbourne."

We usually have no idea when we will die. Death can strike at any time. This is part of Jesus' teaching on death. I certainly don't think it means we are to go around worried and depressed all the time, but we should at least give it some serious thought and be prepared.

At death, we are judged for what we have done

The hardest part of Jesus' teaching on death is about judgement.
He once put it like this:

> The time will come when all of the dead will come out of their
> graves. Everyone who has done good things will rise to life, but
> everyone who has done evil things will rise and be condemned.
> (John 5:28-29)

None of us wants to be judged and certainly none of us wants
to be condemned. Most of us have a built-in mechanism that
assures us, "I'm all right. I haven't done anything real bad."
Unfortunately, we forget that Jesus and the Bible in general
say more about pride than murder, and more about selfishness
than stealing. When I think about it, the selfishness that allowed
me to steal is the same selfishness that encourages me to avoid
helping Buff clean the house. Do you know what I mean?

Kings, beggars, cools, dags, old, young, rich, poor—
everyone, according to Jesus, will be raised up sometime after
death and be judged for what they have and haven't done.

I've got to ask myself, how will I rate?

We can all be forgiven and receive eternal life

The most unique and staggering aspect of Jesus' teaching on
death is that free pardon and eternal life are offered to everyone.
Jesus put it like this.

> I tell you for certain that everyone who hears my message and
> has faith in the one who sent me has eternal life and will never be
> condemned. They have already gone from death to life. (John 5:24)

Instead of the nothingness of the 'die and rot' idea, Jesus
promises life. Instead of the endless trap of birth-death-rebirth-
death in reincarnation, Jesus assures us of God's forgiveness and

of the one certain progression— "from death to life", forever.

I guess the most crucial question we can ask is "How can we have this life Jesus offers?"

Just a shadow

Dr Donald Barnhouse was quite a famous public speaker a few years ago. Sadly, just a few years after he was married, his wife died. His young daughter could not understand why mum had to die. She went to her dad one day and asked, "Daddy, you always told us that Jesus died for us. If Jesus died for us, why did Mummy have to die too?"

He wanted to give her an answer her young mind could understand so he said, "Honey, let me think about it so I can give you an answer that you will understand".

Two or three days later, they were driving to the cemetery for the funeral. As they were stuck in traffic, Dr Barnhouse noticed a large truck in front of them. The sun was shining brightly so that the truck cast a huge shadow across the road.

He turned to his daughter and said, "Darling, if you had to be run over, would you rather be run over by the truck or by the big shadow of the truck?"

In her simple way she answered, "I'd much rather be run over by the shadow because the truck would hurt a lot".

He responded, "Baby, that's sort of what Jesus did for Mummy when he died on the cross. He accepted the truck of God's judgement so that only the shadow went over Mum."

Death is a reality. There is no way around it. But as this story tries to explain, the real pain of death is the judgement that follows. However, Jesus died to take our condemnation away, so that only the shadow will run over us. This is what Jesus meant when he said,

I am the one who raises the dead to life! Everyone who has faith in me will live, even if they die. (John 11:25)

You see, even when we die, it doesn't have to mean condemnation. It can mean life. The billion dollar question then is: Do we trust in God and Jesus? It's not simply a matter of whether or not we believe they exist—most people agree with that. It's a question of trust or confidence. Do we rely on Jesus for forgiveness and eternal life? Do we accept that by dying in our place and then rising again, he absorbed our judgement? If we do, his promise to us is pretty straightforward: "Everyone who has faith in me will live, even if they die".

One Saturday night some years ago, I kissed Buff goodbye and said I'd call in a day or two. The next day I rang to find out that she was sick and couldn't even come to the phone. A day later, I received a call from one of her sisters telling me that Buff had been taken to hospital. I was concerned to say the least.

Over the next few days they did lots of tests on Buff and eventually discovered she'd had a brain haemorrhage and that a blood clot had formed on the right side of the brain. It had to be removed.

Now brain surgery is not the same as having your appendix out. It is often very dangerous. At one stage the doctors informed us that Buff had something like a 60% chance of surviving. I guess that's good, but I couldn't help thinking that it also meant something like a 40% chance of dying.

Buff's mum flew back from overseas; flowers and cards were arriving; all over Australia, people were praying for her. We were all worried—that is, everyone except Buff herself.

The night before the operation I visited her in hospital. She was in a lot of pain and pretty disoriented, but she was not scared. In fact, she seemed more worried about having her hair shaved off for the operation than she was about the operation itself. She figured that if the odds went against her and she died, she'd end up with God, so it wasn't so bad.

As it turned out, Buff's operation was successful. She was out of intensive care in a matter of hours and home after ten days. Within a year she was 100%. Within a couple of years I married her. Looking back, Buff does not recall feeling especially brave or heroic. In fact, she doesn't remember much of it at all! But being with her at the time, I was impressed with her simple confidence that Jesus, 'the expert' in this area, would keep his promise.

Everyone who has faith in me will live, even if they die.

For suspicious minds

1. Try reading the story of the rich man in Luke, chapter 12, starting at verse 13. Why did God call the man a fool?
2. How do you feel about death? Do you ever think about it?
3. How do you think you will rate when your time to die comes?
4. What do you think of Jesus' teaching that free pardon and eternal life are available for everyone?

12

The crook and the Christ

FROM PAIN TO PARADISE

The fact that you have got this far in the book probably means one of three things: you're a speed reader whose brakes failed at chapter five; you dislike most of what I've said but have read on 'cos you love a good argument; or you may be feeling slightly drawn to the message about Jesus and want to know more. Whatever your position, the next two chapters in many ways are the most important of all. If you're looking for an argument, they will annoy you the most. If you're interested in God's friendship, they will hopefully make things clear.

Naked

One of the most significant episodes in Jesus' life centres around his own gruesome crucifixion. It is sometimes overlooked that Jesus was one of three men executed that Friday morning centuries ago. Two criminals were also given the death sentence and were nailed to their own crosses, one either side of Jesus. How strange that the man who would split history into two parts—BC and AD—would end his life in between two common criminals.

Try to imagine yourself in the position of one of those criminals. Nails as thick as your finger have been hammered through the tough part of your hands and through your feet. You're hanging naked on a cross which stands a few metres high and a crowd has gathered a short distance away to watch your final moments.

One of the last things on your mind is the party on Friday night, or the 'break and enter' you had planned for early Sunday morning. You probably couldn't care less that your hair is untidy or that the crowd notice you've put on weight. In every sense of the word, you are naked. You hang there, stripped of all your securities, ambitions, hopes and strengths. There is nothing to hide behind and nothing to bring you comfort.

In reference to a man about to be hanged, someone once said that knowing you are about to die "wonderfully concentrates the mind". In other words, it tends to give perspective and focus to your thoughts. This is undoubtedly what the criminals next to Jesus were experiencing as they hung on those crosses, in agony, struggling to breathe.

Stop and ask yourself: What thoughts would be spinning around in your head in such a situation? What things would seem important to you at that moment?

Amazingly, we have a record of a conversation that broke out between the two criminals and Jesus. Their words tell us lots about what they were thinking and what they saw as important (you'll find the full story in Luke 23:32-46).

Failure

One of the criminals seems to feel nothing but anger and hatred toward Jesus. I guess that's quite understandable, given the circumstances. Think about it. You're ashamed, in a lot of pain and generally feeling spiteful at the world. Next to you is a famous religious teacher who spoke about love and honesty, and who claimed to be the 'Messiah'—that is, the eternal king sent by God to lead us in God's ways. That criminal sarcastically yelled, "Aren't you the Messiah? Save yourself and save us!" Wouldn't you feel a bit resentful toward Jesus?

Meanwhile, something remarkable was happening in the attitude of the other criminal. The emptiness and tragedy of his circumstances forced him to take a hard look at his own life. He yelled back at the first criminal, "Don't you fear God? We got what was coming to us, but Jesus didn't do anything wrong."

I find it astounding that in the midst of his physical pain, sorrow and fear of death, this criminal was concerned about his own guilt and his fear of God. He even spared breath to defend Jesus.

The words "we got what was coming to us" are rarely spoken by a convicted crook. In my 'darker' years, I got into trouble with the police a few times and I don't ever remember admitting my faults to anyone. Many of the inmates in the prisons that I've sung and spoken in are quick to blame others and very slow to admit their own fault. (Even so, I must admit that some of the most down to earth and regretful people I've met have been inmates in Australian prisons.) Still, it's worth pointing out that for this man next to Jesus to admit his own moral failure in front of everyone, he must have been doing some pretty serious soul-searching.

I think we need to ask ourselves: have we ever done this kind of soul searching? Of course, you don't need to be hanging on a cross about to die to take a hard look at yourself. For most of us, our own conscience seems to shine the spotlight on our failures—the things in our lives that we know are wrong.

Albert Einstein developed the theory that gave us the atomic bomb. He was more famous for his scientific achievements than his wise sayings, but he once made a very interesting remark about human nature.

> The true problem is in the heart of man. It is not a physical problem but a moral problem ... It is not the powerful explosion of the atom bomb which frightens us, but the hateful power of the human heart.

It's hard for us to imagine the kind of attitude that starts a nuclear war, but what Einstein called "the hateful power of the human heart" is often just as visible in the playground or in the pub as it is on the battlefield.

Time Magazine ran a series of articles a while back under the heading, 'What's wrong with the world?' There were stories on war and poverty and other problems in modern society, all attempting to answer this age-old question. GK Chesterton, a famous journalist and author, decided to write to the editor:

Dear sir,

In response to your article titled 'What's wrong with the world?',

I AM.

Yours sincerely,

GK Chesterton

Time published the short letter, but I'm not sure how many people actually caught his drift. The problem isn't poverty or war—it's us. As someone said,

The heart of the human problem is the problem of the human heart.

I can relate to this. As I said before, I remember going to my scripture teacher after class and asking: "If God was true—which he's not of course—what would he think of my life?"

Around that time, my soul was bothering me. I thought to myself, "What if God was there? What if he saw my every shortcoming? What if he held it against me?" I was searching my heart. Part of me said, "I've never done anything real bad. It's not as if I'm a murderer." Another part of me replied, "Shut up, Dickson. You know you're selfish. You're proud and you ignore God. Face the truth."

In a much less dramatic way, I felt like the criminal on the cross who looked into his heart and saw his failures. I hope it's not being too forward to ask, have you?

Paradise

Fortunately, the record of this criminal's words doesn't end there. Hearing him admit his own guilt is surprising, but what happened next is staggering. He dared to ask Jesus to save him a place in God's kingdom. Somewhere along the line it must have dawned on him that Jesus was the king, or Messiah, after all. These were his simple and brave words as recorded in Luke 23:42.

Remember me when you come into your kingdom!

What a change of heart! Only weeks before this, he and the other criminal had been living a life of crime. I bet none of his friends would have predicted that in such a short time, he would be looking into the eyes of a famous religious leader, asking for a place in paradise.

Imagine what was going through his mind as he looked across his blood-soaked arm at Jesus and blurted out his request. He must have been wondering, "Will he refuse me? Will he accept me? How could he?"

I suppose Jesus had every right to refuse this man. After all, how can someone live a life of selfishness and then, in his dying hours, feel a bit of regret and expect to be forgiven? If Jesus had responded with a flat 'no', I guess the criminal would only have been getting what he deserved. However, if this story shows us anything, it reveals what kind of man Jesus was and is. Remember, Jesus also had nails through his hands and feet and before being led out to his execution, had undergone vicious torture from the Roman soldiers. Even so, his response to the criminal was crystal clear:

I promise that today you will be with me in paradise.

Jesus' acceptance was instant, complete and with no strings attached. There was no intelligence test, no dress regulations and no age limit. There were no loan repayments, no mention of past sins and no demands to pull the socks up and go to church. This is what makes the life and teaching of Jesus so unique. He didn't offer a method or bunch of rules about how to get on God's side. All through his life he personally and completely forgave the guilty.

Unlike any other

The uniqueness of Jesus was confirmed for me by a conversation I once had with someone from another religion. Some time ago, Buff and I were walking through Circular Quay in Sydney, minding our own business, when a bloke wearing Rayban sunglasses and an Akubra hat walked up to us. Out of the blue he said, "Excuse me, you just walked through a smiling zone and you weren't smiling, so I'm going to have to fine you".

"I beg your pardon?" I said, stunned.

"You just walked through a smiling zone and you weren't smiling, so I'm going to have to fine you", he repeated.

He held up his identification card and explained that he was actually collecting money for the homeless kids of the city and that the smiling zone bit was just an interesting way of getting people's attention. It worked on me.

I gave him the little money I had in my pocket and said goodbye. As we walked off, Buff said to me, "Did you realize he was collecting for the Hare Krishna movement?"

I certainly hadn't. I felt ripped off—not because I've got something against Hare Krishnas but because with his finger, he had covered the part of his ID card that said where he was from.

A few months later, I was again strolling through Circular Quay, minding my own business, when a young woman walked up to me and said, "Excuse me, you just walked through a smiling zone and you weren't smiling, so I'm going to have to fine you".

I paused, smiled and replied, "But joy is much deeper than a smile on the face, don't you think?"

I said it as if it was the first thing that came to mind but actually I'd been planning it for months. You should have seen her face. It was well worth the five bucks I gave the other guy.

I told her I knew where she was from and suggested we talk about her beliefs instead. She agreed and we sat down. For the next half an hour, she described how dissatisfied with life she used to be and that now, in the Hare Krishna religion, she had found fulfilment, peace and love. She spoke of her daily 'mantras' (repetitive prayers which, if recited often enough, hopefully bring you closer to God) and of her efforts to be good in the hope of being reincarnated higher and higher up the ladder.

I eventually mentioned my discovery about Jesus and told her about my rebel years of insistent selfishness and violent attitudes. I explained how at 15, I heard about the God who loved me and who offered me his instant, complete, no-strings-attached forgiveness, like that given to the criminal next to Jesus.

I will never forget that conversation. And I will never forget the look in her eyes as she listened to the story of the God who came to rescue us—the one who doesn't demand constant repetitive prayers or expect us to work our way into his favour. The message of Jesus seemed to amaze her. She looked at me as if to say, "I wish what you're saying was true". I was reminded again that this offer of complete forgiveness is unlike any other.

The story of the crucified criminal and a whole stack of other stories about Jesus remind us that his whole life was one huge rescue mission. People like you and me are the ones he came to save. It's not us reaching up to God trying to prove our 'goodness' (just as well, I think), but it's God coming down to us, demonstrating his kindness. He's done everything needed for us to be his friends. In fact, the only things you and I contribute to our own rescue are the moral failures we need to be saved from! In other words, God's forgiveness is free of charge.

For that dying criminal, Jesus' promise—"Today you will be with me in paradise"—must have been the most extraordinary words he had ever heard. His failures were now forgiven and his pain was soon to be replaced by paradise.

It may seem strange that a common criminal was the first person to witness and experience the significance of Jesus' death, but that's what Christianity is all about. Ever since that first Good Friday, thousands of soldiers, doctors, druggies, bikers, politicians, yuppies, teachers, grannies, mums, dads, students and crooks have looked at their lives, seen their failures and asked God to forgive and forget. And he has.

For suspicious minds

1. The crook on the cross next to Jesus did some serious soul-searching. How would you honestly consider the state of your life before God?
2. Why do you think Jesus was able to promise the crook paradise?
3. What are you going to do personally about Jesus' offer of forgiveness?

13

The dark side of forgiveness

WHEN GOD GETS SERIOUS

"What a load of bull! How can a God who claims to be perfect let a convicted criminal off the hook? Where's the justice in that?"

These questions can be a real problem for some people, and in many ways I completely understand. I mean, without justice, the world would be a mess. Suppose someone in your class cheats in an important exam, gets the top mark and when found out, doesn't get penalised. Or worse, imagine a rapist being caught and then let off with a light 'talking to'. You could probably think of many similar examples.

The question is a good one: if we require justice in our world, why should it be any different with God? Why should God forgive the criminal on the cross? Why should he welcome in a drug dealer who's spent his life ruining the lives of others? Why should he accept a crooked politician after he has lied and cheated to the public? How could he pardon a convicted murderer or a wife beater? Or, closer to home, how on earth can a selfish teenager like me, suddenly at 15, call himself a Christian? Come to think of it, when we evaluate our lives, why should any of us be in the running for a second chance from God?

The answer to these questions is simple: There is actually a dark side to God's forgiveness.

According to the story we've been following, although God's forgiveness was free of charge to the criminal, it was extremely costly to Jesus. It continues like this.

> Around noon the sky turned dark and stayed that way until the middle of the afternoon. The sun stopped shining. Jesus shouted "Father, I put myself in your hands!" Then he died. A crowd had gathered to see the terrible sight. After they saw it, they felt broken-hearted and went home. (Luke 23:44-46, 48)

It's hard to imagine a more unfair execution. Jesus was not a crook, but he died between two of them. He posed no political threat, but it was politicians who sealed his death. He never spoke of a military takeover, but it was soldiers who hammered the nails through his body. On that day, the only truly innocent man of all history was slaughtered like a truly guilty man. But this is precisely the point: one innocent man died in the place of guilty people so that guilty people could become innocent.

When Jesus died, he took upon himself the full force of God's anger. He absorbed our punishment. He endured judgement so that we could enjoy forgiveness. He suffered like hell so that we could get to heaven. The blow we deserved, he took. This is the dark side of forgiveness.

So then, back to the original question: How can a God who claims to be perfect let a convicted criminal off the hook? It is because someone else was put on the hook (so to speak) instead of him. Jesus was condemned in his place.

I remember the day this fact came alive in my mind. The following paragraph in the Bible hit me between the eyes.

> He was despised and rejected by men. He was pierced for our transgressions, he was crushed for our iniquities; the punishment that brought us peace was upon him, and by his wounds we are healed. We all, like sheep, have gone astray; each of us has turned to his own way; and the Lord has laid on him the iniquity of us all. (Isaiah 53:3-6)

When I read this, it suddenly dawned on me that I was literally connected to Jesus' death, even though it happened nearly 2000 years ago. I realised that he suffered, bled and died for *my* slackness and that God's forgiveness was not something to take for granted. It was costly.

Some time ago I heard about a man who, while on an interstate business trip, betrayed his wife and had a fling with a young businesswoman. When he returned home, he debated in his mind whether or not to tell his wife. After a couple of weeks, the guilt got too much. He sat his wife down at the kitchen table and through his tears confessed his unfaithfulness and begged her forgiveness. Understandably, it was a very emotional moment, but despite his wife's shock and hurt, she looked at him and through her own tears said, "I forgive you". He could hardly believe it. It seemed so simple.

A week or so later, this man was sitting in his office thinking about his wife's amazing pardon and he decided to go home, thank his wife and tell her how much he loved her. As he opened the front door of his house he heard crying from the bedroom. He quietly walked over to the door which was slightly open and looked in. There was his wife kneeling by their bed sobbing and repeating, "Lord, help me to forgive. It hurts so much. Help me to forgive …"

As this man stood frozen at the bedroom door he was struck by two thoughts: He realised the greatness of his wife's forgiveness, but it also dawned on him just how much his betrayal had cost her.

Picture Jesus dying on the cross and the same two thoughts should strike each of us. When we understand that Jesus died for your wrongdoing and mine, we ought to be amazed at the depths of God's forgiveness—that he would go that far to get each of us off the hook. But the other thing is that it ought to dawn on us just how much our own betrayal (of God and one another) cost Jesus. God's amazing forgiveness has a beautiful side and a dark, costly side. Great for you and me. Costly for Jesus Christ.

Probably no-one has understood this better than the criminal on the cross. Only a short time after he had been promised paradise, he watched a strange darkness swallow up the sky as Jesus yelled out and died. On the one hand, he must have felt an overwhelming happiness, knowing he was forgiven by God and on his way to paradise. On the other hand, however, watching Jesus sacrifice his life must have been a very, very disturbing experience.

It must have occurred to the criminal that his lifelong selfishness and rejection of God was no joke. His past would have seemed pretty hollow during the moment he saw Jesus die. In fact, if he could have somehow survived the crucifixion and been given a second chance, you could be sure he would have cleaned up his act. His insight into the cost of God's forgiveness, together with his gratitude for that forgiveness, would have been a powerful motivation for change.

As with all the episodes recorded about Jesus, this one has some pretty obvious implications for you and me. We should probably start by asking ourselves a few questions: Do we realise what God's forgiveness cost Jesus? Are we grateful for it? And will it affect the way we live in the future? These questions are crucial if we want to understand Christianity.

In these last few chapters, I've tried to clearly explain the Christian faith. The problem with attempting this is that Christianity is both simple and massive at the same time, which means you can't include everything. It's so simple that a little kid can fully embrace it and yet it is so huge that some of the greatest brains of history have been in awe of it. I hope I've been able to explain the very essence of Christian belief, which is that Jesus Christ died so that everyone can discover a never-ending friendship with God. The story of the crucified crook is perhaps the first and finest example of this discovery.

For suspicious minds

1. Why did Jesus have to die?
2. How can God offer to forgive people who really deserve to be punished? How is that fair?
3. What is the 'dark side' of God's forgiveness?

14

From despair to fear

THE DIFFERENCE A RESURRECTION MAKES

Imagine the devastation felt that Friday when Jesus' followers watched the great man die before their very eyes. Having heard him teach, they were convinced his was a voice of clarity they needed amid all the stupid claims of society. Having seen with their own eyes his ability to heal, they were convinced he embodied the power of God, just as their Scriptures had foretold. The proposition that he was the promised Messiah—God's eternal king—had seemed the only reasonable conclusion.

But now that conclusion seemed ridiculous. There he was, not seated on a throne surrounded by dignitaries, but on a cross, naked and bleeding, surrounded by depressed followers and disinterested bystanders.

We are now a long, long way from the days when thousands hung on his every word, stood amazed at his healings, and pinned hopes on him as the one who spoke and acted for God.

This loss of hope in Christ is seen nowhere more dramatically than in the actions of the women disciples two days after Jesus' death. During his lifetime Jesus had spoken repeatedly about dying and rising again. But somehow the 'rising again' bit didn't sink in. We're told in the Gospel records that on the Sunday morning after Jesus' crucifixion, several of Jesus' women friends bought spices and went to his tomb to 'anoint' his body. Now, you don't anoint a body that you think is about to get up again. This was actually a way of paying your last respects to a loved one. Jesus' crucifixion had so shattered his followers' belief that they were preparing to say goodbye to their lord for good.

These women have given up on Jesus' claim to be the Messiah, the king God sent into the world to lead you and me. Despite all they've seen and heard, they've now put the life of Jesus into the category of a sentimental memory, a story to be cherished, perhaps, but not one you'd base your life on.

I reckon lots of people are like that. They hear a little about this great man—about his teachings, healings, or whatever— but then put his life in the category of a 'sentimental story'.

They catch a glimpse of his greatness but then give up on the possibility of his being as great as he first seemed. They have a sneaking suspicion that Jesus is something special, but for various reasons don't end up pursuing the matter.

Let me give you some examples of what I mean.

I've met plenty of people over the years who used to go to Sunday School or church, or who have fond memories of a past Scripture teacher, but then as the years rolled on and life grew more complex, the 'Christianity' of the past just didn't seem to provide the answers they were looking for. Like the women at the tomb that ancient Sunday morning, they give up on their hunches about Jesus.

Others I know simply have doubting minds. They got a little interested in Jesus but then watched some sceptical documentary raising questions about the Bible or Jesus and suddenly their confidence in Christ goes out the window. Most of us are unaware that the reason sceptical books and documentaries get so much publicity is that they come from the shocking fringes of scholarship rather than the 'boring' mainstream. I mean, the caption 'Scholars affirm the events of Easter' is hardly a sexy headline.

Others give up on thinking about Christ for more psychological reasons. They've seen perhaps that belief in Jesus involves certain lifestyle choices—financial generosity, sexual faithfulness, or whatever—and decided that these are choices they are unwilling to make. Psychologists tell us that when a person's 'belief' clashes with a desired 'lifestyle choice' it is often the belief that gets adjusted or discarded. I've seen mates do just that with Christ.

But whatever real or imagined reasons exist for losing confidence in Christ, the events of the first Sunday after Jesus' crucifixion confront you and me with a very stark reality. And no-one was more powerfully confronted by this reality than the women I mentioned earlier, who turned up at Jesus' tomb expecting to find a dead body. Here's a bit from Mark's Gospel that describes what happened:

> After the Sabbath, Mary Magdalene, Salome, and Mary the mother of James bought some spices to put on Jesus' body. Very early on Sunday morning, just as the sun was coming up, they went to the tomb. On their way, they were asking one another, "Who will roll the stone away from the entrance for us?" But when they looked, they saw that the stone had already been rolled away. And it was a huge stone! The women went into the tomb, and on the right side they saw a young man in a white robe sitting there. They were alarmed. (Mark 16:1-5)

Put yourself in their shoes. You're going to pay last respects to someone you loved and deeply respected. Arriving, you find the grave open, your loved one gone, and a stranger standing there instead. Your first thought would undoubtedly be, 'Someone has trashed the grave!' No wonder the passage says they were "alarmed".

But 'alarm' at the thought of a wrecked grave turns to outright 'fear' at news of a resurrection. The Gospel of Mark continues with these words:

> The man said, "Don't be alarmed! You are looking for Jesus from Nazareth, who was nailed to a cross. God has raised him to life, and he isn't here. You can see the place where they put his body. Now go and tell his disciples, and especially Peter, that he will go ahead of you to Galilee. You will see him there, just as he told you." When the women ran from the tomb, they were confused and shaking all over. They were too afraid to tell anyone what had happened. (Mark 16:6-8)

How strange is this! I would have thought they'd be thrilled: imagine hearing that a departed loved one had returned to life again. There are few things I'd rather in life than to see my dad one more time. I lost him when I was nine years old, but I remember for years afterwards looking out for him in crowds in the childish hope that he was still alive.

And so the reaction of these women is bizarre. They run away, they're confused, they're "shaking all over", and they're too afraid to speak to anyone about it all.

Why 'fear' at the news of Jesus' resurrection? What do the women know that many of us perhaps don't? Put simply: they know the meaning of the resurrection. These women know that this is not simply the return of a loved one. It is in fact the ultimate demonstration of all that Jesus had said about himself for the last few years. For these women, this is the moment when the whole story of Christ crashes in on them: 'The one we ate with, talked with, laughed with, watched die, and even gave up on, *is the Messiah* after all! He is the one sent to show us what God is like and to lead us in God's ways.'

In that moment at the tomb on Sunday morning, all those sentimental ideas about Jesus as the departed loved one pale before the trembling realization that he is in fact the living, almighty one. Sentimentality gave way to faith; mere remembrance was transformed into deep reverence; all the reasons for turning away from Christ now looked pathetic. 'Fear', in the sense of awesome wonder, is exactly the right response to Jesus' resurrection. And, according to the Gospels, when the rest of Jesus' followers saw the risen Christ with their own eyes (in the days following), they too were 'afraid'. They all bowed the knee to Jesus, accepting his absolute power over their lives.

In a way, the resurrection of Jesus should do the same

to us, all these years later. Jesus rising from the dead is not a fairytale. This didn't happen in JRR Tolkien's 'Middle Earth' or in JK Rowling's Hogwarts. It happened in first-century Jerusalem, and the world has never been the same since. Jesus' resurrection calls on all of us to look at the empty tomb (so to speak) and know, with these women, that Jesus is not a lovely memory from the past; he is the risen King of today.

For those whose Christian knowledge stopped growing once they left Sunday school, or gave up on Scripture classes, the challenge is to match your maturing questions with a mature understanding of the relevance of the living Jesus.

For those with intellectual doubts, I guess the obvious question is: for all the 'fringy' anti-Christian documentaries or books you might have come across, have you given as much attention to comprehending the facts about Christianity? I guess this book is a start but believe me, this is 'small fry' compared to most of the excellent material out there explaining the reality of the life, death and resurrection of Jesus. Feel free to email my publisher for a reading list.

And as for those who have perhaps adjusted their thinking about Christ because they think it might clash with certain lifestyle choices, there are at least two things worth pondering. Firstly, are you sure your idea of what Christ demands is accurate? I ask this because I've met a lot of people over the years who have resisted Christianity because of an image in their minds of the prudish, one-dimensional lifestyle that being a Christian is thought to involve. But Christianity makes no such demands. Sure, there are some 'Ned Flanders' Christians in the church. But the church is a big place, open to everyone. You'll find all sorts of people who follow Christ in their daily lives, some nerdy and hung up about all sorts of rules, and most who are just normal people trying to love God and love their neighbours. Whatever you do, don't resist your hunches about Christ just because of some imaginary idea of what it is to be a Christian.

Having said that, secondly, I've been talking to others about this stuff long enough to know that some people have resisted or thrown away their faith because of some *real* conflict between following Christ and certain lifestyle choices. They've looked at Christ's teaching, looked at their desired way of life, and chosen to forget about the former in favour of the latter. I guess in this case I can only ask: is it really worth it? Can anything be so important as to warrant losing a connection with the person who died and rose again for you? Thinking about it purely logically, the answer has to be 'no'.

The resurrection of Jesus is an event that not only changed history, it changed (and changes) lives as well. It gives us a great leader to follow through all the ups and downs of life—one who is alive and kicking and fully able to hear about and help us through our daily issues. It gives us a wonderful 'saviour' who assures us that we are loved and forgiven by God. And it provides us with a promise that beyond death we will experience what Jesus himself experienced—eternal resurrection life.

For suspicious minds

1. How did the resurrection of Jesus affect the women who went to the tomb?
2. What does the resurrection say about Jesus?
3. How do you react to Jesus' resurrection?

15

More than a hunch

OUR SUSPICIONS CONFIRMED

The longer I'm a Christian, the more sense it makes to be one. The faith I stumbled across at 15 is so much larger and more important than I first realised. The cliché is true—life is like a huge puzzle which has to be pieced together. I'm not really into puzzles, but Buff loves them. She even took one on our honeymoon (mind you, that's not all we did for the 10 days). Imagine trying to put a massive puzzle together without the picture on the front of the box to show you what it's meant to look like. Unless you have the picture to explain things, how will any of the little pieces make sense? Of course, if you find the corner bits, you can make a start, but if you're anything like me, you would give up in frustration. You know that all of these little pieces of cardboard fit snugly together to reveal a picture, you have a sneaking suspicion that there is a solution, but you're not quite sure how to find it.

What I'm getting at is this. Knowing God and his Book is like having the front of the box for the giant puzzle of life. It explains what it's all about. It seems to me that the more we learn about our world, the more questions we end up asking and the more explanations we need. Put another way, the more bits of the puzzle we find, the more complex it seems and the more annoyed many of us get. We always suspect that there is some order and purpose and meaning to our lives, if only we had an overall picture of things. If only we had the front of the box, then things would be different.

In a way, this book has been an attempt to introduce you to the Big Picture, like showing you the front of the puzzle box. We started by examining the parts of life which lead us to suspect that there is something in Christianity. In the first chapter, I talked about sex and how some of us are attracted to what we think is 'sexual freedom', only to sadly find that a cheap 'Datsun' view of sex can make it hard to develop stable, meaningful relationships. God, on the other hand, has a 'Porsche' attitude toward sex. If only more of us looked to God and what he says to us in the Bible—there we'd discover what sex is about and how fulfilling it can be.

We looked at fashion and the media and how image-obsessed some of us are. Some of us devote our lives to striving for the right image, but few of us ever achieve it. Even those who do, the pop stars and super-models, soon discover that it doesn't provide the security and happiness they're seeking. If only more of us had taken Jesus seriously when he said, "Isn't life more important than clothes?"

I tried to look head-on at our moral failure. It's not a pretty subject I know, but it hits home for most of us. The majority of us have a hunch about what is right and wrong and that we don't always measure up, but few people take it any further. Jesus came like a doctor, diagnosing our problem but also offering some medicine. Although he didn't have a psychology degree, his explanation of human nature was frighteningly accurate.

Jesus didn't come simply to tell us to pull our socks up and be good. He didn't just understand human nature; he claimed he could transform it. On one occasion, he described us as 'slaves' to selfishness and then promised he could set us 'free'. Either he was completely arrogant or he was telling the truth. I described the surprise I got when I found that God could actually change me and that Jesus was for real. Over the years, I've met heaps of people who seem to have been literally 'freed' by Jesus to be kind, self-controlled and strong in character. It's far more than just 'turning over a new leaf'. A real transformation seems to have taken place. In a society obsessed with 'self-help' books, I wish more people looked to Jesus as the great transformer. I believe we would then slowly learn how to get along with each other in this strange world of ours. The puzzle would begin to make sense.

Some people, of course, reject all this 'religious' talk, arguing that science has rid us of God and given us hope for a better world. In chapter 5, I attempted to explain why I am sure this is far from true. I don't doubt that we've been greatly helped by modern discoveries, but even many scientists are happy to agree that science is unable to find answers to the big questions of life: Why are we here? Does our life have real value and purpose? How can life become fulfilling? Jesus, on the other hand, does tackle these issues.

Then there is the piece of the puzzle that doesn't quite fit—the puzzle of suffering. We're surrounded by injustice and sorrow. We always had a sneaking suspicion that something was drastically wrong with life and the suffering around us seemed to prove it. Even if our life is fairly together, we're still confused about the pain we see in other people's lives. I hope that I have encouraged you to see that Christianity both points to an answer to this terrible question and brings comfort to all of us who suffer.

We also looked at other religions and how some people are confused by the range of views on offer. Some give up hope of finding any answers at all because there are so many religions and philosophies, each claiming to be authentic. You might remember that I described how Jesus was like God's photo, showing what God is like. Unlike other religious leaders, he claimed to be the personal image and revelation of God. He told his disciples that when they looked at him, they could see God.

The final chapter under 'nagging doubts' looked at whether God would accept us if we just tried to live a 'good life'. We saw how this very common Australian view doesn't take account of just how high God's standards are. We could never be good enough to make God's team. We're better off learning to rely on his forgiveness.

In this last section of the book, I wanted to shift our focus from our suspicions and doubts about life to what I believe is the guts of it all. The message of Christianity gives us hope for this life and beyond. According to Jesus, death is not the scary mystery that many of us think it is. It can be the entrance into something incredible. Jesus was always on about 'eternal life'. He never described it as fairies and angels floating through the air playing harps and listening to choir music. He likened it to a huge party, full of good food and drink, surrounded by great company—God especially. For the Christian, there is great reason for being hopeful about the future.

So then, what does the puzzle I've been raving on about look like? What is the picture on the front of the box? Well, you have already seen it. You read about it in the last few chapters. If this imaginary puzzle was completed, it would undoubtedly reveal a man dying on a cross. Jesus' death makes all that I've been talking about possible. Without him dying, we could never enter into the life God offers us and we could never see things through God's eyes. In a society which seems so lacking in forgiveness, Jesus bursts onto the scene and dies to take the just punishment that we deserve. In our society, if you stuff up, you pay. But Jesus assured us that, regardless of how we've lived in the past, God can forgive and forget. His death for us is the guarantee.

There is one more piece of the puzzle that actually makes the whole picture relevant to you and me right now. Quite simply, the Jesus who died, is alive to this day. As we saw in chapter 14, after Jesus' brutal execution he was literally raised to life—not in fairytale land, but in reality. If we had been at the right place at the right time, we would have seen Jesus alive from the dead with our own eyes. But here is the great thing. Although Jesus' resurrection took place so long ago, the fact that he is alive, means that all this Jesus stuff is relevant to us today. The Jesus who spoke, laughed, healed, forgave and died is alive (now in heaven) right to this moment. This means that we can connect with him in our daily lives. Jesus' resurrection takes the picture of the puzzle and turns it into a living, breathing reality.

The longer I'm a Christian, the more sense it makes to be one. As far back as I can remember, I've always had my suspicions that there is more to life than Coke and Reeboks, or beer and footy, or fashion and entertainment. I've also always had a hunch that God had something to do with it all. At age 15, all my suspicions were confirmed. Jesus captured my attention and imagination. His life, death and rising from the grave just captured me and I thought, "I want to follow him".

I wrote this book to explain Christianity to you. I wanted to simply set out what it means to be a Christian so that you can make an intelligent, informed decision about whether or not you too want to follow Jesus. I don't kid myself that I can change your mind or 'convert' you. That's not my job. Where you go from here is up to you. You may not be willing or ready yet to pursue these things any further. But I hope you will not just go through life without ever thinking deeply about your sneaking suspicions.

On the other hand, you may really feel drawn to Christ and want to go further. If that's you, let me encourage you to go for it. Find a Christian you know and ask them to help you out. I'm sure they'd be more than happy to point you in the right direction. You might like to find a church where you belong. There are a lot of good ones. Get hold of a modern version of the Bible and have a read for yourself—the Gospel of Mark in the New Testament is a good place to start. But above all, talk to God. Tell him you want his forgiveness, his coaching, his life. Talk to him like you would anyone else that you respect and admire. He is ready to hear you and involve himself in your life. He is ready to confirm all your suspicions.

If all this is more than a hunch for you, I've included some more stuff on the next page to show you how to take it further. You don't have to read it, but if you want to make Jesus more than just a suspicion, by all means, read on.

God bless you heaps!

For suspicious minds

1. Think back over what you've read in this book. Has it confirmed your suspicions? Has it answered your doubts?
2. What are you going to do next?

16

Where to from here?

I've always found it tricky answering the question, "How exactly does someone become a Christian?" because there's always the danger of making it sound mechanical, like enrolling in university or filling out a job application. There are not 'three-quick-steps-to-God' or 'a-hundred-and-one-ways-to-be-religious'.

Becoming a Christian is far more like beginning a friendship than joining a club or applying for a course. It's all about new relationships—with God and with his people.

Marriage is probably as good an illustration as any of what it means to be a Christian.

When I married Buff there were certain things that had to be in place to make it meaningful. Firstly, I had to know, love and respect her. In a similar way, being a Christian involves these elements. Knowing that we've disobeyed God but that he sent Jesus to die and rise so we could be forgiven. Loving God for all he has done for us. And respecting him as creator of the world, and the one true ruler, coach, or father of our life.

But the marriage illustration goes further. There was, of course, a point when I committed myself to Buff for life. The wedding promises I made to her weren't just meaningless tradition but a moment of true commitment. Likewise, for all of us there can be a moment of true commitment to God which might begin with a prayer like the following. The words aren't magic, but hopefully they are helpful as an example of how to turn to God:

Dear God,

I know I've ignored you and rebelled against you.

I realise I deserve your punishment.

But thank you for sending Jesus to die for me so that I could be forgiven.

Thank you that he is alive again.

Forgive me for all that is past.

And teach me to follow your lead from now on.

Thanks again.

Then, of course, just as in every marriage there is the daily effort to please the other partner, so being a Christian involves the daily attitude of putting God first: searching out what kind of life he wants us to live and then applying it to our situation at school, uni, work, family, sport, friendships and everywhere.

Can I challenge you to read the Gospel of Mark? My book may have been helpful to you, but you will get the most complete picture of Jesus from reading the original documents.

And, finally, I'd be short-changing you if I didn't leave you with one more suggestion—*meet with other Christians.* To be honest, it's hard to describe how much I've benefited from speaking with, listening to, and spending time with other Christians at church, over meals, at parties, on the phone … A church in your area, of your choice, is a great place to start.

Anyway, thanks heaps for reading my book. I hope that some of your own suspicions have been confirmed along the way and that these last few thoughts help clarify where to go from here.

Feedback on this resource

We really appreciate getting feedback about our resources—not just suggestions for how to improve them, but also positive feedback and ways they can be used. We especially love to hear that the resources may have helped someone in their Christian growth.

You can send feedback to us via the 'Feedback' menu in our online store, or write to us at PO Box 225, Kingsford NSW 2032, Australia.

Matthias Media is an independent Christian publishing company based in Sydney, Australia. To browse our online catalogue, access samples and free downloads, and find more information about our resources, visit our website:

www.matthiasmedia.com.au

How to buy our resources

1. Direct from us over the internet:
- in the US: www.matthiasmedia.com
- in Australia and the rest of the world: www.matthiasmedia.com.au

2. Direct from us by phone:
- in the US: 1 866 407 4530
- in Australia: 1800 814 360 (Sydney: 9663 1478)
- international: +61 2 9663 1478

3. Through a range of outlets in various parts of the world. **Visit www.matthiasmedia.com.au/information/contact-us** for details about recommended retailers in your part of the world, including www.thegoodbook.co.uk in the United Kingdom.

4. Trade enquiries can be addressed to:
- in the US and Canada: sales@matthiasmedia.com
- in Australia and the rest of the world: sales@matthiasmedia.com.au

Hanging in There

John Dickson's first book is a survival guide for the young Christian (aged 13-20), dealing with basic subjects like:

- living with parents who aren't Christians
- the dilemma of doubts
- too much too young—about sex and stuff
- hanging in there—the key to remaining a Christian.

One of the most widely read Christian books in Australia in the last 20 years, and with good reason!

A Hell of a Life

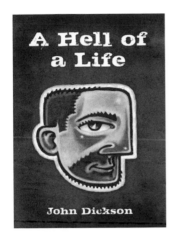

This popular youth book by John Dickson focuses on the radical life of Jesus. With clarity, simplicity and an engaging style, John explains that the life, death and resurrection of Jesus has supreme and abiding relevance for everyone. Jesus' life was full of action, danger, mystery and power. Yet the focus of his whole life's work was to die. In doing so he took Hell for us, so that we wouldn't have to.

FOR MORE INFORMATION OR TO ORDER CONTACT:

Matthias Media
Telephone: +61-2-9663-1478
Facsimile: +61-2-9663-3265
Email: sales@matthiasmedia.com.au
www.matthiasmedia.com.au

Matthias Media (USA)
Telephone: 1-866-407-4530
Facsimile: 724-964-8166
Email: sales@matthiasmedia.com
www.matthiasmedia.com